WOMEN, CHILDREN AND POVERTY

WOMEN, CHILDREN AND POVERTY

By

Dr. M. LAKSHMI NARASAIAH,

Professor and Head,
Dept. of Economics,
Sri Krishnadevaraya University Post-Graduate Centre,
Kurnool—518 002 (A.P.)

DISCOVERY PUBLISHING HOUSE

NEW DELHI—110 002

First Published-2001
Reprinted-2011

ISBN 81-7141-580-6

Published by
DISCOVERY PUBLISHING HOUSE
4831/24, Ansari Road, Prahlad Street,
Darya Ganj, New Delhi-110002 (India)
Phone: 3279245 • Fax: 91-11-3253475
E-mail:dph@indiatimes.com

Mehra Offset Press
Delhi

Preface

Poverty has always been with us and for atleast forty years its alleviation has been the professed objective of many strategies to improve the lot of the Indians. But the way in which it has been conceived, however, has been subject to considerable change. Relatively little attention was paid to the development of the poor themselves. Rather, they were portrayed as among the beneficiaries of development in larger systems which were to provide the dynamic force for the elimination of poverty (from the "outside" as it were). Development was principally something that happened to the poor—on a "trickle-down" basis.

The simple assumption that the poor would benefit from general economic growth, without paying any special attention to them, changed somewhat in the late 1950s, when it was perceived that the poor might not automatically benefit from macro-economic development, but that they must benefit if the social stability needed for overall economic growth was to be assured. From this point there emerged a specific line of antipoverty thinking to improve the income of poor people.

The manner in which the poor were to be integrated into the overall growth process, however, was very specific. It was concerned not so much with what the poor could offer to the growth process—as with what they should receive from that process. For all its merits the Basic Needs strategy, and the social "safety net" approach which followed it, basically emphasized the consumption needs of the poor—and not their surplus producing possibilities. On the contrary, a persistent theme in the discourse about the economics of the poor has been the need for some sort of transfer of resources to them from more productive and dynamic sectors of accumulation. In short, the poor have been portrayed as a net burden on the growth process.

It is possible to introduce an element of differentiation into this picture: given that it is rarely alleged that low wages are an obstacle to accumulation and growth, the poor who have been characterized as a burden have tended to be those not directly integrated into nascent large-scale systems of production: these are the poor "peripheral" to modern economic process—a group which encompasses a large proportion of the urban population in India (principally employed in the "informal" sector), as well as a vast mass of small, but relatively independent agricultural producers. Implicitly, then, the concepts of "peripheral", small-scale and poor have been run together to form, in the realm of ideas, a more or less dependent mass. The number of people ostensibly in these categories is huge, and they seem to represent an enormous burden on development. They represent a development "problem", and an awesome one at that.

While substantial progress has been made in India in reducing the percentage of the rural population below nationally defined poverty line, the absolute number of the rural poor has increased. The growth of output did not bring about a significant improvement in the income share of the lowest nor an uniform reduction in the percentage of the rural population below the poverty line. The situation actually worsened. Less than half of the rural population in India has access to safe water or sanitation, and only 60 per cent had any access to health services. National data on life expectancy, infant mortality and literacy show improvements, but also the persistence of completely unacceptable conditions.

Author

Contents

1

Rural Poverty in India

"It is morning in a remote farming area in India. As her husband harnesses a bullock to plough their field, a woman pounds the grain she will use for the day's main meal. Three kilometres away, their children are collecting fuel wood and water before starting their morning walk to school".

"After school, they help their mother light a fire with a few sticks, milk the cow and collect the sundried grain. That evening, as the family rests around the hearth, father worries about how to sell his onions before they spoil and the price falls. Before sleeping his wife prepares a basket of home-grown vegetables to sell next day at the village market five kilometers away. With the takings, she hopes to buy a kerosene lamp although she might not have enough cash left to buy the kerosene immediately...".

That description of rural life is a daily reality for hundreds of millions of families throughout India. Rural poverty means subsistence on the meagre earnings of wage labour or unreliable harvests from small plots of land. It means raising a family without safe drinking water or proper sanitation, suffering disease or injury without medical assistance. In times of un-employment or crop failure, it means living with the pangs of hunger—and the risk of death by famine.

Inside the Poverty Trap

Poverty in rural India is created and perpetuated by a number of closely interlinked socio-economic processes.

1. Policies and institutional arrangements biased against the poor exclude them from the benefits of development, frustrate their productive potential and accentuate the impact of other poverty processes. Institutional processes that perpetuate rural poverty include lack of access to land, inequitable share cropping and tenancy arrangements, poor markets limited access to credit, inputs and technology, and ineffective extension services. Other constraints are lack of training facilities, inadequate research related to smallholder farming systems, and last but not least a lack of grassroots institutions needed to foster people's participation.

   Policy and institutional biases have short and long-term impacts. In the short term, the poor are unable to earn enough to meet nutritional requirements or to take advantage of the market. "In the longer term", "poor households continue to lag behind because they do not generate a surplus for investment, nor do they have access to investment opportunities. Moreover, the rural poor may be forced to overuse resources, which undermines productivity and income".
2. Even today dualistic agrarian structures originating in colonial times persist. In India, highly capitalized large and medium-sized farms have virtually monopolistic control over land and

labour at the expense of the small farm sector. Large scale commercial producers—control the best farm land. Resources have been funnelled into irrigated plantations producing cotton and mechanized cultivation of sorghum. In marginal areas, mechanization has led to environmental degradation and the loss of seasonal grazing and stock routes for pastoralists.

"Thus, side by side with modern agriculture, millions of marginal farmers and herdsmen subsist far below the poverty line". This dualism severely limits their capacity to grow food and accumulate capital. They lack marketable surpluses, and incentives and opportunities to save and invest.

3. Rapid population growth can cause and perpetuate rural poverty by increasing pressure on limited productive resources, social services and employment, as well as—paradoxically—creating labour shortages through outmigration.

   The most obvious consequence of rapid population growth is that, even with relatively high rates of economic growth, improvements in living conditions are limited. Total saving in the economy declines, leaving fewer resources for investment in human development. Negative consequences are most acute in rural areas. Growing population often combined with traditional laws of inheritan—has led to fragmentation of holdings, degradation of crop and pasture land, and falling yields. In areas with unequal distribution of land, rapid population growth has accelerated proletarization of the rural work force and reduced incomes.

4. Rural poverty malnutrition and undernutrition are closely linked to environmental degradation. Poor people in marginal areas are destroying natural resources as they struggle to keep their production systems sustainable. In acute shortage of arable land has forced farmers to reduce the length of fallow

periods and plough up land previously reserved for grazing. These practices have led to declining yields, soil depletion and further impoverishment. Population pressure is pushing weaker members of the rural community into ecologically vulnerable areas.

Degradation of the environment is strongly linked to household food insecurity and lack of fuel. Much of the fragile forest cover has been destroyed by poor rural people in the search for grazing land and fuel wood.

Government policies have also wrought environmental damage. A rapid expansion of areas under crops often accelerates deforestation and land degradation. Programmes to expand cereal production into marginal areas, subsidized capital to support commercial operations subsidies for inappropriate technologies and excessive transfer of income out of the agricultural sector may undermine the sustainability of smallholders and pastoralists production systems.

Inadequate public investment in off-farm employment and infrastructure, a lack of price incentives and inadequate access to modern agricultural inputs and services discourage investment in land conservation, leading to further overuse and degradation.

5. As poverty undermines traditional social bonds, the marginalisation of women has become a fact of rural life in India. With little or no access to land, millions of women depend on casual employment on meagre wages. Often, they farm fragmented plots of poor quality, Limited access to inputs, extension, training and credit limits in turn, their ability to enter commercial agriculture.

The exodus of males in search of work in urban areas (itself and indicator of poverty) has serious consequences for the women they leave behind. Output from land often falls and less attention is paid to maintenance, setting the stage for a long-term decline in productivity. Many female headed households have abandoned the use of oxen for ploughing, some plough and plant late and others no longer weed their fields.

6. The ethnic or cultural marginalization of tribal or minority populations also plays a role in poverty. Many of these groups are further threatened by newly marginalized groups as the expansion of cultivation reduces the grazing areas of nomadic herders.

7. Exploitative middlemen also perpetuate rural poverty. Landlords exploit share croppers and tenants, moneylenders exploit debtors, and traders exploit small scale producers. During seasonal food shortages, the poor may have to borrow money at interest rates exceeding 20% a month. Forced to devote most of their energies to debt servicing, they sink deeper into the poverty trap.

   In some cases, government controlled cooperatives and government agencies whose task is to protect the poor may themselves practise forms of exploitation. Heavy levels imposed by government agencies have damaged small farmers. Large, inefficient bureaucracies are paid for by the productive sectors of the community and frequently contribute to the accumulation of large budget deficits.

8. Political troubles and civil strife have had a disastrous impact on the rural poor one effect is the disruption of development assistance to the rural poor, both from national and international agencies. Another is the transformation of many producers into consumers of social services, with serious

consequences for production, savings, capital accumulation and investment.

9. The international economic environment directly influences the well-being of the Indian poor. Falling commodity prices and protectionist policies in India affect the employment and incomes of plantation workers and small-holders producing for export, particularly those relying heavily on a few agricultural commodities. Changes in international interest rates have repeatedly hurt small scale producers in debt-burdened India, while world grain price increases has triggered rural famines.

   The net flow of development resources to agriculture also affects rural poverty. Official development funding for food and agriculture increased between 1975 and 1982, but has fluctuated irregularly since. Moreover, concern with trade balances is diverting resources to export crops, sometimes at the expense of traditional crops grown by poor farmers.

2

The Persistence of Indian Poverty and its Alleviation

Poverty has always been withus and for atleast forty years its alleviation has been the professed objective of many strategies to improve the lot of the Indians. But the way in which it has been conceived, however, has been subject to considerable change. Relatively little attention was paid to the development of the poor themselves. Rather, they were portrayed as among the beneficiaries of development in larger systems which were to provide the dynamic force for the elimination of poverty (from the "outside" as it were). Development was principally something that happened to the poor—on a "trickle-down" basis.

The simple assumption that the poor would benefit from general economic growth, without paying any special attention to them, changed somewhat in the late 1950s, when it was perceived that the poor might not automatically benefit from macro-economic development, but that they must benefit if the social stability needed for overall economic growth was to be assured. From this point there emerged a specific line of antipoverty thinking to improve the income of poor people.

The manner in which the poor were to be integrated into the overall growth process, however, was very specific. It was concerned not so much with what the poor could offer to the growth process—as with what they should receive from that process. For all its merits the Basic Needs strategy, and the social "safety net" approach which followed it, basically emphasized the consumption needs of the poor—and not their surplus producing possibilities. On the contrary, a persistent theme in the discourse about the economics of the poor has been the need for some sort of transfer of resources to them from more productive and dynamic sectors of accumulation. In short, the poor have been portrayed as a net burden on the growth process.

It is possible to introduce an element of differentiation into this picture: given that it is rarely alleged that low wages are an obstacle to accumulation and growth, the poor who have been characterized as a burden have tended to be those not directly integrated into nascent large-scale systems of production: these are the poor "peripheral" to modern economic process—a group which encompasses a large proportion of the urban population in India (principally employed in the "informal" sector), as well as a vast mass of small, but relatively independent agricultural producers. Implicity, then, the concepts of "peripheral", small-scale and poor have been run together to form, in the realm of ideas, a more or less dependent mass. The number of people ostensibly in these categories is huge, and they seem to represent an enormous burden on development. They represent a development "problem", and an awesome one at that.

While substantial progress has been made in India in reducing the percentage of the rural population below nationally defined poverty line, the absolute number of the rural poor has increased. The growth of output did not bring about a significant improvement in the income share of the lowest nor an uniform reduction in the percentage of the rural population below the poverty line. The situation actually worsened. Less than half of the rural population in India has access to safe water or sanitation, and only 60 per cent had any access to health services. National data on life expectancy, infant mortality and literacy show improvements, but also the persistence of completely unacceptable conditions.

The pursuit of growth has not solved the development problem. Trickle-down has not worked or it has not worked enough. The massive persistence of poverty, particularly in rural area represents a problem for the popular acceptance of continued economic adjustment; and it represents a problem for growth itself. The problem lies not only in the unintended consequences of the prevailing development paradigm, but in the viability of the paradigm itself. Part of the debt crisis arose from an inability to mobilize fully domestic assets, and from systematic resort to external resources. The unsustainability of this form of development has been amply demonstrated. Part of the answer to the challenge of development lies in a greater and more appropriate use of the resources of developing countries themselves.

A substantial part of these assets can be created by the poor who have been so marginal to past development efforts. The poverty of a nation and the poverty of people are not as easily separable as was often thought in the past. In many cases, it is difficult to envisage national growth without strong development among the poor themselves—not as objects, but as subjects of development. The fact that this is insufficiently perceived is as much an expression of the development of social and economic interests as it is of the development or otherwise of economic theory. Development has frequently been associated with large-scale production and large-scale inputs of capital, and these new social and economic patterns have often defined development in their own image, i.e., in terms of the centrality of large-scale production and accumulation.

Poverty Alleviation

The perspective is not that growth achieved by the better-off will pull the poor out of poverty, but that the mobilization and enhancement of the resources and activities of the poor themselves can uphold their dignity and free them from the shackles of misery, while at the same time making a vital contribution to overall sustainable growth.

Individually and collectively, the obstacles facing the poor are formidable. They are, however, not insuperable. Most of the forces creating poverty are essentially social. They reflects systems of resources allocation that are made by societies, and as such they can be reversed. Pricing policies, credit systems, and social and productive services which neglect the poor, as well as gender discrimination, are not natural, universal and inevitable facts—and neither is the poverty they give rise to. One of the major obstacles to overcome in fighting poverty is the perception of poverty itself—and of the poor. In this regard, perhaps the most important point is that the poor are not idle, they work. Nobody is simply "poor". In other words, it is not just a state of being. In this regard, "poor" is more aptly used as an adjective rather than as a noun. The rural poor are poor farmers, poor herders and poor fishermen. In short, they are poor producers: their incomes are gained from their work. The answer to poverty lies in creating the conditions for them to earn more from their work. From this perspective, overcoming poverty does not mean less growth, it is a contributor to growth—for it means making the poor more productive. Too often in the past poverty alleviation has been seen as a burden on the economy, as involving a transfer of something for nothing in exchange. It need not be that way: it can be an investment in production, benefiting both poor and the national economy. Poverty has been defined as a production problem, and poverty alleviation as an investment.

Nobody wishes to be poor, and few accept it passively. The poor are rarely without initiative. What they lack are the means of pursuing it. In no small measure, overcoming poverty involves building upon this initiative and will, helping organize cooperation, and providing material support. This support does not have to take the form of handouts. The problem of the poor is not that they cannot handle resources efficiently, but they do not have access to them.

The challenge of creating an institutional framework for credit for the poor is an expression of the general institutional challenge facing poverty alleviation: institutions are not oriented to the poor. Many factors enter into this, ranging from the costs of working with a large number of unorganized people, to the prevalence of 'myths about the improvidence of the poor, to a simple desire on the part of the better-off to monopolize scarce resources. The answer to this is to create institutional responsiveness, either through introducing demand-led organization into existing institutions concerned with the poor or through promoting institutions created by the poor themselves. In both cases, participation by the poor is critical. The objective is not only to mobilize the individual initiatives of the poor, but also to mobilize their collective strength and capabilities. As individuals, many of the poor are virtually unreachable. As members of associations and groups they create their own channels for institutional access.

The poor as producers; the poor as credit-worthy handlers of material assistance; the poor as institutional actors—these are not elements of theory, but of practice and experience. Notwith standing the growing acceptance of the need to do something "about" the poor, not everyone shares this understanding of poverty. As long as the poor are viewed from after, the myths of poverty and the poor persist. Even those who overremphasize the need for social "safety nets" and handouts, while ostensibly helping the poor, maintain the image of helplessness, and of the need to do something "for" them. A closer view reveals something very different: tremendous work and initiative on the part of the poor, both based on their desire to do something for themselves. This is not a burden, it is an extraordinary social and economic asset. Again, viewed from a distance, poverty looks overwhelming. The closer view reveals very specific situations of opportunities and needs. These can be responded to—not only through soup kitchens, which should be seen as desirable in addressing emergencies only—but through strengthening the individual and collective means available to the poor to carve out their own path of independence and growth. The dynamics of poverty are reversible, but only in collaboration with the poor themselves.

Precisely because of past neglect of the poor as producers, a neglect involving a failure to involve them in the process of technological development, organization, and capitalization, the gap between the current and potential production of the poor is enormous. Investment in the poor is not a loss-making enterprise. Poverty is less a failure of the poor, than a failure of policy-makers to grasp their potential. Far from there being a tradeoff between poverty and growth, the persistence of poverty represents a limit to growth.

Mobilizing and enhancing the ability of the rural poor to expand their own income and contribute to national growth is not simply a process of raising incomes. It involves structural change in economics and societies. It involves helping the poor to position themselves securely within main-line economic processes. This means first increasing and improving their access to land—by land reform, land-titling, better management and better conservation, supported where necessary by irrigation, new technologies and improved infrastructure. Secondly, it means increasing the productivity and use of rural labour, emphasizing labour intensive technology and better training for new skills. Thirdly, it means making more capital available to the rural poor, mobilizing savings, providing infrastructure and developing financial services tailored to their situation and needs.

Not least, it means acknowledging the important contribution of poor women in all of these areas of activity. At present, the contribution of women to the rural economy is seriously underestimated—the "invisible women" syndrome. Official statistics rarely make any effort to measure it, even though it is more than clear that not just unpaid household work but the farm and trading activities of women make a vital and significant contribution to the well-being of poor rural households. All the evidence suggests that the poorer the household the more hours women work and the greater their investment in both economic production and family welfare. From a situation of multiple disadvantage as poor, as women and often as single parents, women can move to one in which they contribute and benefit three—fold—in the home, in society at large and, not least, in the development of the next generation.

Many of the measure that need to be taken to allow the poor to realize their potential do not involve more expenditures; they involve the elimination of economic distortions against the rural poor. These distortions have effectively taxed the poor, and mainly the rural poor, in favour of inappropriate and inefficient urban developments whose support has been at the root of widespread economic crises. To no small extent, helping the poor make their potential contribution to development involves no more than creating a "level playing field" and, when conceived in such a light, structural adjustment can make a vital contribution to both resumed growth and social equity. It is often felt that the poor are somehow "outside" the scope of national economic policies. This is virtually never the case. They are affected by national economic policies, but this inclusion takes a very special form: exposure to the costs, and exclusion from the benefits. In this regard, there is a certain irony in the view that small-scale producers "need" subsidies to survive. In fact it has been the development of large-scale production in agriculture (and industry) in India that has been heavily dependent upon subsidization over the decades—benefits which small-scale producers have rarely enjoyed.

This is characteristic of many forms of large-scale production in India—although nominally at the cutting edge of efficiency and productivity, it is they rather than the small-scale producers who have been dependent upon transfers and protection for their reproduction.

Change in the environment of poverty necessitates greater awareness of the root causes of poverty on the part of policy-makers. However, the realization of the social and economic potential of the rural poor is not just a question of economic policy and investment. It also involves the development of a general social framework in which the economic and social interests of the poor can be freely articulated and responded to. It means, instilling democratic and participatory values at every level in society and not just at the level of nationwide institutions. The most valid spokesmen of the poor are the poor themselves.

The opening of economic and social opportunities to the poor offers the possibility of more stable and sustainable change. The alternative is for societies to polarize further, for the welfare burden to grow to greater proportions and for a widening gap to develop between the modern and traditional sectors. In the end, the continued poverty of the rural areas will be a brake on the output of the advanced sector, eroding the potential for self-sustaining growth.

3

The Dynamics of Rural Poverty in India

Poverty is homogeneous only when considered from the point of view of income or consumption: the uniformity of the poor as a category exists only on the level of the fact that they have little to consume. When considered from the point of view of production, i.e., the circumstances in which the poor must operate to gain their income, the conditions of poverty are extraordinary diverse. A concrete grasp of these diverse circumstances is the first step in developing relevant instruments to address not only the problems of the poor, but also the challenge of taking advantage of the opportunities available to them.

The conventional means of measuring economic progress, such as Gross National Product per capita, tell us little about the real nature of poverty. In recent years this sort of yardstick has been supplemented by measurements of food security, income distribution, and social development (encompassing health and education). These offer the possibility of composite indices, allowing the development of more rounded characterizations and comparisons of poverty at the national level. However, these principally refer to the symptoms of poverty, not to the relational factors generating it. Poverty is not a state of being, it is the effect of dynamic processes. While it is important to know where poverty is greatest, it is critical to know why it exists. This inquiry necessarily leads away from the nature of the poor as individuals to the nature of their social and physical environment. Poverty is not only a personal phenomenon, it is a social status. As such, while its effects can be measured on the level of the individual, its causes must be sought elsewhere. From the point of view of poverty alleviation the process of becoming is just as important as the state of being.

At the heart of poverty is the inadequate access of the poor to productive resources. Low incomes tend to reflect inadequate means of production, not in incompetent producers. However, poverty in India is not simply a reflection of private resources. A broad range of "external" factors impinge on incomes, among them the following:

National Policies

One of the ironies of Indian development is that while no government wants poverty, many policies contribute to it—what is given in anti-poverty programme is drained away by other policies. The poor do not always come out ahead in the balance—they are often net "donors" to the rest of society. Frequent reference is made to unsustainable forms of development—to urban over-expansion, industrialization based on subsidies, and to public sector engorgement. What is less frequently realized is that the bill for these phenomena is often presented to the rural poor.

Taxation of exports to sustain sectors with little export potential of their own and subsidized food imports to supply the urban population are policies that are often paid for by the rural poor. In many areas of India, exports are agricultural goods produced by small farmers. Here export taxes contribute to rural poverty. The same is true of "cheap" food imports which depress the prices paid to small farmers for their food crops.

"Structural imbalance" is not only a recipe for increasing external indebtedness, it is also a recipe for increasing the poverty of the rural population. The political weakness of the poor in most areas is not only the basis for inadequate poverty alleviation programmes and policies—it is the basis for an actual transfer of their income to more socially influential groups. While it is often correctly asserted that the poor are the first to suffer from adjustments involving public social expenditure cuts, it is often the case that they also have the most to gain from the elimination of policy-based economic distortions that reflect social power rather than productive efficiency and potential.

Demographic Factors

Accelerated population growth is a long-term contributor to poverty. In India the incomes of the poor have declined, mortality rates are also falling, pushing the numbers up. In the meantime, land is becoming scarcer, plots more fragmented and the soil and pasture increasingly degraded. This phenomenon is not without its policy dimensions. As long as the poor remain undercapitalized, and essential determinant of household income is the amount of labour available to it household economic strategies favour large families. While population policy has a role to play, possibly more critical is a change in the economic environment. Access to capital and more secure income changes perceptions of the need for labour. In the medium and long-term, population dynamics are driven by the underlying productive systems. As long as the production systems of the poor remain underdeveloped, population growth remains high, restricting even the future possibility of development.

Natural Resource Management and the Environment

If poverty is both cause and effect of rapid population expansion, so poverty is both cause and effect of many dimensions of degradation of the environment. Many of the rural poor, but by no means all, live in areas of extreme environmental fragility, a circumstance often prompted by high level of control by the better-off over more stable and productive resource areas. Here the poor are extraodinarily exposed to the dangers of erosion, whittling away at an already meager productive base. The threat is not entirely due to nature. Rather, poverty accelerates erosion. Without capital, the poor are frequently unable to invest in even traditional methods of soil and water conservation. And without sufficient land they are forced to shorten fallow periods, putting further strain on the resource base. As in the case of population growth, the result is strain not only on the poor, but on the entire Indian economy. Given the extremely limited economic alternatives, the solution to this problem is not to forbid the use of environmentally fragile resources to the poor, it is to change the conditions under which their use takes place. Access to conservation technology is important; but more so are security of land tenure and resources to invest.

Combating poverty means not only increasing the production of the poor, but also preserving and enhancing the long-term value of the resource they control. What this very often means, in practice is assisting the poor in reestablishing a stable relationship with fragile resource. Prevailing processes in many areas involve the gradual—and sometimes not so gradual-depletion of natural resources, to the detriment of all. Part of the answer to this is conservation. Part of the answer is also to provide viable economic alternatives to the poor, reducing their dependence on erosion-prone crop and livestock practices.

Exploitative Intermediates

The poor are not unaware of the pressure upon them, and also of means of overcoming them. Their ability to respond, however, is serverly impaired by social powerlessness. The poor are surrounded by a dense network of public and private factors reducing their freedom of action, and actually draining what few resources they do have. Members of the network include traders and moneylenders capitalizing upon the economic weakness of the poor, and engaging them in unequal exchanges. They also include public agencies either indifferent to the requirements of the socially uninfluential, or actively engaged in extracting "surplus" for us by other groups. Not to be excluded from this are organizations which are ostensibly "for" the poor, but which, in fact, serve as systems of containment and control.

4

Employment and Poverty Alleviation

Today the key socio-economic problem is large-scale enemployment. Spreading joblessness brings many other problems in its wake. It erodes national incomes and living standards, aggravating the already grindingly difficult job of promoting development and alleviating poverty. Joblessness also raises government budget deficits, increasing macro-economic instability while soaking up investment for productive capital expenditure, education, training and relief aid. And joblessness ruins lives and communities by depriving people of the dignity and satisfaction that comes with earning one's keep and making a contribution to the well being of family and society.

Theories about how best to nurture development (and thus create jobs) have shifted considerably over the last decade. The state role has evolved, in the minds of many, from being a source of relief for the problems of unemployment, poverty and underdevelopment, to being a fundamental cause of these problems through the distorting impact of its intervention on the market.

However, the more market oriented philosophy that grew up during the 1980s has yet to provide convincing solutions in practice at least not on a grand scale and especially not in terms of job creation as the present jobless economic recovery demonstrates.

The weakness of the current recovery and past approaches to economic development can be traced to the failure to consider employment as the predominant means of promoting growth and alleviating poverty. In policy circles it has too long been an almost ignored priority.

Current trends thus bode poorly, particularly as unemployment rates soar. In light of the circumstances, we need to begin re-examining some of the fundamental questions if only to find out what has gone wrong with the answers.

Minimum wage?

Let's begin with wages. With corporate restructuring in full force on a global scale, are low wage rates required to raise employment and maximize profits? A top manager of a multinational consumer electronics group certainly thinks so; he likened the perfect factory to a ship "so that we could move it around the world to where labour was cheapest". Perhaps, but this bottom-line emphasis on unit labour costs ignores at least two other factors; namely, that higher wages can act as a screen to select more productive workers and that higher wages translate into better productivity via improved worker nutrition, increased consumption and a generally healthier quality of life.

If higher wages bring these benefits (and it is an open question) should government insist that there be a minimum wage rate? Neo-classical economists tend to respond "no", assuming that a higher wage rate puts money into the pockets of some low wage workers while forcing many others out of work because companies cannot afford to pay them.

Technology Transfer

The impact of technology is another area in need of study. Technological innovation is usually labour-saving and tends to originate in industrialized countries, moving toward developing countries like India, Pakistan where labour tends to be low cost and abundant. Would it therefore make sense to slow down or somehow restrict technology transfer, especially to development markets, in the interest of preserving employment?

The answer here is clearly—no. Historical evidence abundantly demonstrates that attempts to retard technological progress bring about greater poverty and lower growth. Technology, infect, is at the heart of the new endogenous growth theory which is very much in vogue among development economists today. Slowing down or inhibiting technology transfer would certainly dash many countries' development hopes and aggravate poverty. However, the relationship between technology, development, employment and poverty alleviation is not without its complications.

In the 1970s, the buzz word among development specialists was "appropriate technology", i.e., small-scale and labour-intensive technologies that would increase productive output while allowing an equilibrium solution to be found such that the ratio of the productivity of labour to that of capital is proportional to their relative prices. The conditions for this "small is beautiful" approach to technology tended to be best met in agricultural production. However, where manufacturing industry is concerned, the small-is-beautiful approach foundered badly when the only viable technological alternatives proved to be highly capital-intensive.

Development Gap

A wide gap has emerged between developing countries with an inward focus (which tended to be protectionist and pursue policies of import substitution) and those with an outward focus and a policy of pursuing export-led growth. Competing in international markets requires technology that is as good as or better than that found in advanced, industrialized nations. Small, therefore, is not beautiful in the global manufacturing economy where product standards are high and the elasticity of substitution between labour and capital is very limited.

The drive to obtain state-of-the-art technology thus leads to a policy conundrum: it is a pre condition for success in manufactured exports, but the impulse to compete successfully in this most lucrative sector speeds up the transfer of technology from the developed to the developing world, thus reinforcing the bias toward labour saving equipment in developing countries and accelerating a process that is seen as a source of job loss in the industrialized countries.

Technology and Jobs

Before concluding that modern technology transfer is inimical to employment in developing countries, we have to distinguish clearly between technology's static and dynamic consequences. In a static sense, it is true that highly capital-intensive export industries may not create much employment on a net basis, but the dynamic effects of technology transfer do contribute to economic growth. And growth, in turn, generates multiplier effects in the form of demand, which stimulates ancillary production activities (like food processing or consumer goods) that rely on more labour-intensive technologies.

The problem is that the diffusion and application of technology on a global scale blurs the categories of international product specialization and creates a much more competitive and conflict-prone international environment.

For example, we have already seen the Asian Tigers move from producing goods such as textiles and processed food to producing hi-tech and value-added consumer durables. This advance is only possible due to the growth of human capital (facilitated by investment and higher incomes) and it leaves production of textiles to other industrializing countries, like Indonesia, the Philippines and now China. But the dynamic comes at the expense of jobs in industrialized regions, like the US and the EC, which lost more than a quarter of their work force in textiles during the 1980s. Inspite of job losses, advanced countries continue to produce textiles, notwithstanding major differences in the hourly wage rates for spinning and weaving and the fact that essentially the same hi-tech equipment is being used in most production centres.

Protectionism

What has happened in textiles is happening in other industrial sectors (automobiles, for example) as well. The intense market competition is proving to be a source of trade conflicts, and possibly protectionism, as jobs come under increasing pressure.

For many workers and managers, the benefits of foreign direct investment look increasingly like a zero-sum game for employment, and there is a real risk that the tenuous link between overall growth and employment will break down altogether. It is hardly surprising that we are already seeing negatively affected workers and local businesses clamouring for protection in advanced countries.

Governments role

The concerned governments are suppose to carry out much of this research. The three initial lines of inquiry follow from three reasonable assumptions about the future.

- First, increase in welfare and consumption subsidies are out; investment in training and human capital are in. How can investments in human capital be directed to positive employment effects? Is it perhaps not time to explore more fully benefit schemes targeting the unemployed and the unskilled poor providing them with the type of subsidies that would enhance their human capital, improve their health and productivity through better nutrition and preventive medicine, and restore the dignity of holding a job?
- Second, given the quasi-inevitability of increased automation in manufacturing, how can other sectors (particularly

agriculture and services) be developed to export their long-term potential for employment creation?

- Third, given the inevitable pressures of work and productivity in the global economy, what sort of alternative institutional arrangements need to evolve with respect to industrial relations, employment and work conditions?

Finding answers to these and other questions will require no small amount of new thinking, but parochialism or a failure of imagination would be fatal flaws in this global era.

5

Overcoming the Poverty in India and the Lessons Learned

Basic elements in the struggle against poverty in India are the provision of the economic services and assets which the poor have tended not to receive in the past—as a result of oversight or design. The exphasis on economic services and assets is just because the mass of the rural poor are self-employed, and it is upon the improvement in the means of production directly accessible to them that their prosperity depends. Health and education are very important, but offer more if combined with the material means of making a living—of putting body and mind to work. These assets and services include land, water, technology, commercial services, handling output and inputs, and credit—provided within an economic policy framework conductive to their optimal exploitation.

This list is hardly new. It corresponds to the requirements of any producer. The basic points to be made in this regard are: firstly, that the general requirements of poor producers are precisely the same as those of other producers and that measures to alleviate poverty that fall short of recognizing the full range of such requirements are doomed to failure, and secondly, that these assets and services are not typically provided in a form accessible to the poor. India has made important progress in providing a more effective framework for agricultural production "in general", this framework has not properly embraced small and poor producers. They are as follows:

Access to Land and Water

In the case of access to land, for example, land reform efforts in India has frequently involved major loop-holes, allowing the socially powerful to minimize de facto improvements in the condition of the poor. In the critical area of land rights, registration processes have been so complex and costly relative to the resources of the poor that land regularization programmes have, sometimes unintentionally, become virtual characters for legalizing the eviction of the poor and the actual loss of their traditional rights. Irrigation without specific measures to defend the interests of existing occupants of areas exposes them to expulsion—and moreover, has tended to be concentrated in large-scale schemes benefiting already high potential areas in which the better-off predominate. While huge sums have been spent on large-scale irrigation schemes, little has been spent on water conservation and the sort of small-scale developments that are more likely to be or relevance to marginal small-scale producers.

Technology Transfer

In the area of technology, attention has been focused on technologies (such as the Green Revolution) requiring extensive access to water and fertilizers, neither of which are generally available among the poor. In fact, research almost every-where has concentrated on large-scale production in areas of relatively high resource endowment. In contrast to this, research relevant to small-scale producers in marginal soil and rainfed areas in India has been shockingly deficient. As in other fields, this is partly explicable in terms of a frequently unproved belief that large-scale production is more efficient. It is also explicable in terms of the fact that it is the powerful who set the research agenda, not the poor. Taking its inspiration from highly specialized, large-scale agricultural units of production, research has tended to dwell separately on individual crops—rather than on the interaction between crops, which is of much greater relevance to small-scale producers engaging in highly complex systems of production to maximize food self-sufficiency and minimize risks.

Commercial Services

In the area of handling of output and inputs, organized services (not infrequently under public control in the past) have tended to concentrate in the proximity of large-scale producers and users of input in relatively well-endowed areas. In India the poor have had to incur the extraordinary costs of handling their own transport of goods to and from service points—frequently over long and deficiency lines of communications. The alternative has been to resort to private intermediaries offering goods, and buying products, at prices very different from those enjoyed by larger producers. In effect, the better-off and the poor have confronted different sets of prices—with the poor paying more for what they buy, and receiving less for what they sell.

Credit

In the area of credit, the situation has been disastrous. It is generally recognised that productive improvement needs a change in means of production—new tools, improved seeds, fertilizers, etc. Such a change everywhere is typically effected on the basis of credit. Yet rural credit schemes in India have usually not extended support to small farmers and the poor. Credit has been concentrated among richer farmers with collateral, and with demand for larger loans. In order to improve their productivity, the poor have been forced to seek credit from informal money lenders—at virtually confiscatory rates. Again, the cost of modernization has been much higher for the poor than for the better-off. The inevitable result has been a lower rate of change—and the consolidation, rather than the reduction of poverty.

The Victims Blamed

Although vast amounts of money have been invested in rural development in India, very little of it has reached the poor. The poor have been left to their own devices, while the better-off have received a wide range of assistance—not infrequently allowing them to encroach further upon the land of the poor. Support for agricultural expansion has not led to rural development, and it has not eliminated rural poverty. The relatively undynamic performance of many small-scale farmers under these circumstances is frequently taken as "proof" that they are a poor investment. This is a variant of "blaming the victim". In fact, the poor have fared badly, not because they could not efficiently use support, but because they did not get it.

In other words, the failure of the poor to benefit from agricultural sector investments has not reflected and economic failure among the poor themselves. Rather, it has involved policy and institutional failures. On the policy level, it has tended to reflect and unwillingness to restrain the socially influential from seeking to monopolize scarce resources to their own benefit—and, perhaps, a lack of awareness of the incompatibility between apparently "neutral" criteria for support (e.g., the demand for land title as collateral for credit) and the particular circumstances of poor and small farmers (e.g., involvement in traditional forms of land tenure). On the institutional level, it has involved both unwillingness to give weight to the requirements of the poor, and a lack to initiative in solving real problems in providing services to the poor such as the high cost of providing services on an individual basis to a large number of small and often dispersed "clients". While there has been a great deal of lamentation about poverty in India, remarkably little has been done to change it at the level of economic systems—perhaps because social welfare activities are much easier to implement than real policy and institutional changes. It is possible to do very much better—not by simply pouring in more resources (in channels which at times do not even ultimately reach the poor), but by changing the framework of investment, i.e., the instruments of development.

LESSONS LEARNED

Targeting of Resources

The fundamental lessons learned are that investment resources must be targeted at the poor. In a world of competition for scare resources, investments in rural development tend to be captured by those with national and local power—a group which rarely encompasses the rural poor. The first step in delivering resources to the poor is establishing strict criteria for eligibility for assistance. Indicators of wealth in India vary according to the nature of the local economy—in some cases it is extent of land ownership, in others size of cattle herds, in yet others ownership of drought animals—but the principle remains the same: investment in those with the least assets. In some cases, for example, where women represent a significant proportion of actual producers, this may give rise to entirely new patterns of investment.

Reorienting Institutions

The intention to distribute resources to the poorest is not always accompanied by actual performance. Among the reasons for this is the inappropriateness of delivery mechanisms. Put simply, institutions long oriented to the non-poor have tended to develop operating procedures and structures which reflect the nature of their de facto clientele and which hinder them from serving a new target group. In the area of credit, for example, insistence upon collateral in land may be an absolute obstacle to participation by the poor—just as a limited banking network may represent an obstacle to delivery to the poor, for whom the costs of communicating with a bank at considerable distance might well add significantly to the real cost of credit. Effectively channeling resources to the poor, therefore, means the elaboration of institutional means of delivery consistent with their circumstances.

However, it must be recognized that there are exceptional institutional costs associated with providing services to (and among) the poor—costs arising from the fact that there are many individuals involved, and that their individual requirements tend to be quite small. The costs of government services in, for example, agricultural credit, are necessarily higher if this involves a very large number of small producers than if it involves a small number of large producers. Administration costs in banking tend to be much higher relative to loan volume if it involves a myriad of individual small loans. There factors have often been adduced as reasons for the "impossibility" of serving the poor. Effective Service appears financially impossible, especially the context of widespread retrenchment in public expenditure under structural adjustment programmes. The poor are often willing to pay the actual costs of services—especially if the alternative is no service at all, or supply by local informal monopolists. On the other hand, there are proven ways of reducing costs of service supply to the poor—by involving the poor themselves. Everywhere in India poor people overcome some of the obstacles involved in their individual poverty through cooperation and joint action. While such organization typically develops in the absence of formal service organizations and markets, it can also develop in association with formal organizations. In effect, the organized small farmers can help shoulder the cost of services through organizing local level distribution and administration themselves.

People's Participation

People's participation is, therefore, not only a "social" concept. It is an eminently economic concept, involving cost sharing. It is fundamental to the sustainability of improvements. The long-term solution is not to throw money at the problems of the poor, but to help them to organize to overcome themselves. One of the happy externalities of this approach is not only lower cost services, but services more likely to be in harmony with what small farmers perceive themselves as needing.

Balance Development

Development means change, not only in the volume of production, but in the composition of output and the conditions under which it is produced. What is argued is that the pursuit of development without the inclusion of the mass of small-scale producers and the poor has important structural drawbacks, and that their inclusion offers the basis for more sustainable long-term development. Some smallholder groups have a vast unutilized potential for expansion. Others have much more modest prospects.

Even those with the poorest assets and possibilities, however, can be helped to improve their condition. While the direct economic benefits of this maybe relatively slender, the side-effects may be great. An eventual shift of these groups to other areas and systems of production might be inevitable if aspirations for a better life are to be satisfied, but it is essential that this shift be orderly necessitating that support be given in the transitional period. This support can be either a direct welfare transfer or an investment in productive capacity. In many cases the latter may be the least-cost alternative.

The issue, then, is neither the "rich way" nor the "poor way". What is required is: an unprejudiced evaluation of the capacities and possibilities of poor and small-scale producers, and their potential role in the overall scheme of national development; allocation of investment resources according to potential and within an institutional framework ensuring delivery and profitable use; and a more balanced view of the overall social costs and benefits of alternative means of addressing transitional states. The belief is that the outcome of this will involve a reappraisal of the role of the poor in economic development, and a major improvement in the state of the rural poor throughout India.

The poor are many, their productive potential is great, but in few places is the exploitation of this potential an explicit focus of policy concern and action—although everywhere it is the concern of the poor themselves. While concrete evidence of the efficacy of systematic policy of support to the poor is sparse (simply because it has so rarely been tried), the evidence of its effectiveness on the local level is abundant.

6

Rural Poverty in India and Development as a Policy Challenge

Poverty can be overcome, and that the poor can increase their income and production within an appropriate framework. Part of that framework is made up of a flow of resources and local-level institutional development, and there is considerable scope for improvement in both. However, the impact of investment and organization is strictly determined by the nature of the policy environment. While project and programmes can bring some relief to the rural poor, substantial change needs a strong policy commitment. While the poor can overcome poverty, they will not be able to until this becomes a major focus of national policy and action. In the main, this sort of commitment has not been made in the past—at the expense of both the poor and overall development in many areas.

The current state of India is highly contradictory. On the one hand, there is proclamation of a new order; on the other, increasing value is given to sectional and short-term national and group interests. With an overt concern with the India's poor goes an equal weight given to concern with economic mechanisms and relations that pay little attention to poverty and foster more inequality. The dangers of this situation are real. The lack of concrete attention being given to change will mean greater economic polarization. Greater polarization among the better-off, and between the better-off and the poor—means instability and a lack of consensus, a lack of legitimacy.

Poverty is far-reaching, and ought to be curtailed. In a period in which resources everywhere appear restricted, this seems not to be an attractive proposition at the practical level. Welfare is every where giving way to production as an imperative, just as public expenditure is giving way to private accumulation. Poverty alleviation does not appear to be an idea whose time has come. The objections are great, but they are also misplaced. Poverty alleviation is not necessarily a drain upon accumulation, and it is not primarily a public activity. Poverty alleviation is primarily the activity of the poor themselves, and their progress necessarily involves productive expansion. If this potential for private expansion has not been realized, it is not because of the nature of the poor, it is because of the way in which national economic affairs have been organized. Economic policy has been oriented towards the better-off—not infrequently at the expense of the poor. Given the historic association between wealth and power, the definition of development in terms of the large and the wealthy is hardly surprising.

There is the possibility of associated growth involving both large-scale and small-scale production, the better-off and the poor. The realization of this possibility might result from a new social compact. This social compact is not a commitment to social safety nets and welfare, both of which seem to presuppose that the poor are somehow necessarily out of the growth field. It is a commitment to abolishing artificial and onerous terms of exchange that discriminate against the poor, to investing resources where there are real opportunities for gain, irrespective of whether the economic agents concerned are rich or poor, and to creating the space for the poor to organize to pursue their social and economic interests.

Thee is a need for a new growth model consistent with new social realities. While the 1980s was period of clearing away many of the obstacles to development, it was not a period in which there emerged a clear vision of what represented the positive basis for growth, beyond, that is, a general prescription of market-driven operations. The model must pass from admonition to positive prescription to fuel growth by integrating the poor in their rightful place in the production function. It must redefine the position of public expenditure in the development process, and seek to establish market structures which are both equitable and open to the participation of the economically weaker elements of the population. Most of all it must revalue the position and contribution of the poor and small-scale producers in the growth process, particularly in the agricultural sector, but not exclusively agriculture.

This means that the issue is not so much one of less government, but of government, both national and local, finding a new rationale for action, including, *inter allia*, creating conditions that will effectively unleash the productive potential of the rural poor.

Financial flows to the poorest Indians are not likely to undergo a very major expansion, especially through private channels.

Development will rely very much on the mobilization of their own resources, and many of these resources are in the hands of the poor, are indeed, not only the human capital embodied in the poor but also their assets which, while small, individually are cumulatively important in India. The growth model for the 1990s will have to embrace that fact, and build upon it. The paradox of most development models is that they have emphasized the value of what Indians do not have, while devaluing what they have: capital intensity has been promoted in situations of scarcity of capital, at the expense of abundant labour and of low-cost methods of manifold increase of the productivity of assets of which the poor do dispose. In a not very indirect way, the creation of poverty has been subsidized. Poverty alleviation is neither a special topic nor a low-cost substitute for growth. It is neither more nor less "social" than development in general. It is part of the formulation of any sustainable strategy of economic development. In the 1990s it may, and perhaps should, become the dominant issue—not as an alternative to the structural recognizations of the 1980s, but as a means of filling a growth framework with substance.

7

Peace and Poverty

Peace should not be understood in military terms, like absence of armed conflicts. Peace should be understood in a human way in abroad social, political and economic way. Peace should mean social justice between nations and within nations. It should mean establishment of human rights for all people.

In the new context the concept of "peace" would be the existence of a political and economic environment where each individual human beings is truly free; free from the control of any powerful person or any powerful nation, free from poverty, hunger and indignities, each individual human being free to explore the limits of one's own potential.

Today peace is threatened, more than anything else, by poverty, unjust social and economic order, absence of democracy and environmental degradation.

The cold war cloud has gone. You can feel the breath of fresh air around the world. Now there is no visible competitor left for capitalism. It is quite risky to live with a philosophy which has no challenger. To be safe, we must go to the essence of the philosophy of capitalism rather than be satisfied with the practices which emerged over years through patchworks of expediency.

Contrary to common belief, it is not the "free enterprise" which is the essence of capitalism. It is the freedom of individual thought and freedom of individual action which is the essence of capitalism. It is these freedoms which support free enterprise, free trade, free circulation of capital, and free circulation of people.

We must work out a new system, appropriate for the new world, from the basics of capitalism, not from the practices of capitalism. Many of these practices take away freedom, rather than guarantee it. Traps must go. People cannot remain trapped in places where they cannot live because of ecological, political, or economic reasons.

This planet belongs to all people. If some people are trapped somewhere, we must all come forward to remove the causes of their discomfort. At the same time we must leave our shores open for anybody who decides to join us, or any body who decides to part our company.

Poverty denies a person control over his destiny. Poverty means not being able to tell what tomorrow would be like. If we examine the situation carefully we'll see that the poverty is neither created by the poor, nor sustained by the poor. It is the system of policies and institutions that we have built around us that creates and sustains poverty. Poverty is the denial of human rights. Over one billion people live below the absolute poverty line right now on this planet, are denied of almost all human rights. There is no way one can defend the existence of poverty anywhere. Poverty is a disgrace for the entire man—kind. Because we allow another human being to die of hunger, or malnutrition, or common curable diseases, or exposure to climate, we are reduced to less human beings. If a particular world system is responsible for creating this massive poverty we must act to replace it.

Resource-wise or technology-wise, there is no reason why poverty should exist and continue to deepen and widen. If we make up our minds to wipe out poverty from the surface of the earth, the worst aspect of poverty can be removed within the next couple of decades.

We can build a poverty-free world at a fraction of the cost of what we spend on war preparations. Nations become very generous when it come to making their war-machine heftier in the name of ensuring "peace". Can we persuade ourselves to allocate a part of our time, money and intellect to achieve peace by making the people at the bottom the winners, rather than nations winning wars? "Peace" achieved by winning wars is earned by destroying people. The real peace can be achieved by building people, by reinforcing people, by helping people to reach their potential. Removing poverty is the process of building people.

Each human being is a wonderful creation of the Creator. Each human being is born with great potentials. Poverty denies any opportunity for a person to achieve any of his/her potential. We have built a world system which is in the habit of pushing people down not building them up. It creates barriers around individuals, rather than remove them.

The most effective step that we must take to remove poverty is to create a system which creates enabling conditions for people and remove the existing barriers. The institutional barriers were skillfully crafted over the centuries to benefit a handful of people.

Resource-poor nations with high incidence of poverty waste away enormous human capability each day by denying poor people the use of their energy and ingenuity. If they could have been made economically active, not only they could have contributed in the national production, they would have helped expand the domestic market for the products produced. The poor can be transformed into the engine of growth if we only allow them to unleash their capacity.

We cannot be at peace with ourselves if we know there is a human being who lives a life worse than an animal. A human being is supposed to live differently than an animal. He/she is supposed to live a life with human dignity. Human dignity is what distinguishes a human being from an animal. When we cannot ensure this dignity for others, our own dignity becomes an empty pretense.

There must be a thousand and one ways to remove poverty from the earth. We may or may not know some of those ways already. Obviously there are many more ways yet to be designed, each more effectively than others. When we shall find them, how many of them we shall find, how quickly we find them, will depend on how eager we are to find them. But to say that poverty cannot be overcome, directly and quickly, is to underestimate the capacity of human mind.

Poverty is homogeneous only when considered from the point of view of income or consumptions the uniformity of the poor as a category exists only on the level of the fact that they have little to consume. When considered from the point of view of production, i.e., the circumstances in which the poor must operate to gain their income, the conditions of poverty are extraordinary diverse. A concrete grasp of these diverse circumstances is the first step in developing relevant instruments to address not only the problems of the poor, but also the challenge of taking advantage of the opportunities available to them.

The conventional means of measuring economic progress, such as Gross National Product per capita, tell us little about the real nature of poverty. In recent years this sort of yardstick has been supplemented by measurements of food security, income distribution, and social development (encompassing health and education). These offer the possibility of composite indices, allowing the development of more rounded characterizations and comparisons of poverty at the national level. However, these principally refer to the symptoms of poverty, not to the relational factors generating it. Poverty is not a state of being, it is the effect of dynamic processes. While it is important to know where poverty is greatest, it is critical to know why it exists. This inquiry necessarily leads away from the nature of the poor as individuals to the nature of their social and physical environment. Poverty is not only a personal phenomenon, it is a social status. As such, while its effects can be measured on the level of the individual, its causes must be sought elsewhere. From the point of view of poverty alleviation the process of becoming is just as important as the state of being.

At the heart of poverty is the inadequate access of the poor to productive resources. Low incomes tend to reflect inadequate means of production, not incompetent producers. However, poverty in India is not simply a reflection of private resources. A broad range of "external" factors impinge on incomes, among them the following:

National Policies

One of the ironies of Indian development is that while no government wants poverty, many policies contribute to it—what is given in anti-poverty programmes is drained away by other policies. The poor do not always come out ahead in the balance—they are often net "donors" to the rest of society. Frequent reference is made to unsustainable forms of development—to urban over-expansion, industrialisation based on subsidies, and to public sector engorgement. What is less frequently realized is that the bill for these phenomena is often presented to the rural poor. Taxation of exports to sustain sectors with little export potential of their own and subsidized food imports to supply the urban population are policies that are often paid for the rural poor. In many areas of India, exports are agricultural goods produced by small farmers. Here export taxes contribute to rural poverty. The same is true of "cheap" food imports which depress the prices paid to small farmers for their food crops.

"Structural imbalance" is not only a recipe for increasing external indebtedness, it is also a recipe for increasing the poverty of the rural population. The political weakness of the poor in most areas is not only the basis for inadequate poverty alleviation programmes and policies—it is the basis for an actual transfer of their income to more socially influential groups. While it is often correctly asserted that the poor are the first to suffer from adjustments involving public social expenditure cuts, it is often the case that they also have the most to gain from the elimination of policy-based economic distortions that reflect social power rather than productive efficiency and potential.

Demographic Factors

Accelerated population growth is a long-term contributor to poverty. In India the incomes of the poor have declined, mortality rates are also falling, pushing the numbers up. In the meantime, land is becoming scarcer, plots more fragmented and the soil and pasture increasingly degraded. This phenomenon is not without its policy dimensions. As long as the poor remain undercapitalized, and essential determinant of household income is the amount of labour available to it household economic strategies favour large families. While population policy has a role to play; possibly more critical is a change in the economic environment. Access to capital and more secure income changes perceptions of the need for labour. In the medium and long-term, population dynamics are driven by the underlying productive systems. As long as the production systems of the poor remain underdeveloped, population growth remains high, restricting even the future possibility of development.

Natural Resource Management and the Environment

If poverty is both cause and effect of rapid population expansion, so poverty is both cause and effect of many dimensions of degradation of the environment. Many of the rural poor, but by no means all, live in areas of extreme environmental fragility, a circumstance often prompted by high level of control by the better-off over more stable and productive resource areas. Here the poor are extraordinarily exposed to the dangers of erosion, whittling away at an already meager productive base. The threat is not entirely due to nature. Rather, poverty accelerates erosion. Without capital, the poor are frequently unable to invest in even traditional methods of soil and water conservation. And without sufficient land they are forced to shorten fallow periods, putting further strain on the resource base. As in the case of population growth, the result is strain not only on the poor, but on the entire Indian economy. Given the extremely limited economic alternatives, the solution to this problem is not to forbid the use of environmentally fragile resources to the poor, it is to change the conditions under which their use takes place. Access to conservation technology is important; but more so are security of land tenure and resources to invest.

Combating poverty means not only increasing the production of the poor, but also preserving and enhancing the long-term value of the resource they control. What this very often means, in practice is assisting the poor in reestablishing a stable relationship with fragile resource. Prevailing processes in many areas involve the gradual—and sometimes not so gradual—depletion of natural resources, to the detriment of all. Part of the answer to this is conservation. Part of the answer is also to provide viable economic alternatives to the poor, reducing their dependence on erosion—prone crop and livestock practices.

Exploitative Intermediates

The poor are not unaware of the pressure upon them, and also of means of overcoming them. Their ability to respond, however, is severely impaired by social powerlessness. The poor are surrounded by a dense network of public and private factors reducing their freedom of action, and actually draining what few resources they do have. Members of the network include traders and moneylenders capitalizing upon the economic weakness of the poor, and engaging them in unequal exchanges. They also include public agencies either indifferent to the requirements of the socially uninfluential, or actively engaged in extracting "surplus" for use by other groups. Not to be excluded from this are organizations which are ostensibly "for" the poor, but which, in fact, serve as systems of containment and control.

8

After the Microcredit Summit: How to Implement its Anti-Poverty Strategy

More than 2500 people from 100 countries gathered in Washington in February, 1997, to participate in the Microcredit Summit. The goal of the organizers of the Summit is to reach 100 million poor families around the world with microcredits and other financial services within the next ten years. As there are at least six people in a family, 600 million people would benefit from access to micro finance. This means that half of the people in extreme poverty could have the opportunity to get out of their misery.

The fact that more than one billion people in the world are still living in extreme poverty is a sign of failure of our development policy and a scandal for human society. Now there is no longer any excuse. We have learned in the last years that microcredit is one of the best tools to eradicate poverty. At the Summit, there was a consensus between politicians, practitioners, donors, scientists and NGOs on how to reach this goal. Particular emphasis is given to strengthening poor people in their capacities. It is also understood that lack of funds is only one aspect of the most pressing problems in the field of microfinance.

The Approach

The overall goal can be achieved by designing and establishing an appropriate and sustainable institutional framework on the national level in the developing countries. The most significant elements within a feasible strategy to achieve the goal are the following:

- Decentralized bilateral fund-raising and financing under commonly accepted standards are preferred. Whereas the creation of a newglobal facility as a supranational mobilizing and channeling mechanism for microcredit should not be pursued.
- The focal point of the future strategy should be the creation and the support of independent and recipient countries which will operate under the basic principles of outreach. Moreover, the mobilization of domestic funds will be of particular importance. Promoting agencies as wholesale institutions should identify and assess eligible microfinance institutions on the basis of a widely accepted set of performance criteria, identify institutional weakness and requirements at national level and execute programmes for the funding, institutional strengthening, training and linking of participating institutions.

* The NGO Results, which helped organize the Microcredit Summit, will perform as a catalyst in creating public awareness regarding the crucial role of microfinance in poverty alleviation in donor as well as recipient countries.
* The Consultative Group to Assist the Poorest (CGAP) will be responsible for the creation of promoting agencies at the

national level. The role of CGAP will be the monitoring and coordinating of promotional activities. It will act as a platform for setting consistent standards for the operation of individual programmes.

The Next Steps

Under the guidance of CGAP, interested donor and recipient countries should immediately begin to discuss the institutional profiles of promoting agencies and performance criteria of participating institutions. Moreover, the necessary operational procedures for the functioning of the institutional framework at the wholesale level need to be defined by CGAP. CGAP should identify promoting agencies within the next six months. It will be responsible for the coordination of funding activities. Capacity building for promoting agencies as well as for recipient institutions will be a crucial issue. A pilot phase in a small number of countries should be designed to gain experience with the proposed institutional framework in order to develop it further and also determine the adequate volume of funding for potential recipient institutions. Bilateral donors should support these activities.

9

Link Between Disability and Poverty

Disability affects nearly every fifth household in developing countries and is a prevalent contributing factor to family poverty.

An already poor household has an added financial burden when a disabled family member is not involved in productive activities. In the context of extreme poverty, a disability may sometimes turn into an asset when the person uses begging as a way to bolster the family income. But this is a degrading path that does not lead out of poverty.

What aggravates the situation is the fact that poverty is identified as one of the main causes of disability. This is especially so for those at the lowest strata of society who live in precarious conditions without education, hygiene and health care.

An important element of measures aimed at families living in absolute poverty is that they learn how to prevent disability. They must also learn that a disabled family member can take part in economic activities.

Increasing the economic usefulness of a disabled household member can help to reduce the poverty of many families. The income earned by the disabled person not only benefits him or her but the entire household as well.

However, anti-poverty strategies which target disabled household members without attempting to alleviate general household poverty would likely be futile.

One widespread misconception is that disabled people are unable to earn a living and to be self-reliant. As a consequence, disabled people are often targeted only for passive measures of income replacement and social welfare schemes. Active measures in their favour are conceived of as social activities and not economically relevant. Such misconceptions generate and reinforce exclusion, which in turn perpetuates poverty.

This highlights a dimension of poverty often overlooked by economists. They define poverty only in terms of household income. But poverty also means to lack social status and to lose human dignity.

Thus a basic criterion for an anti-poverty strategy at the micro-level is whether it serves to establish human dignity. An approach which merely dishes out state subsidies or international aid to the destitute keeps the recipients in a position of dependence.

Targeting specific groups for poverty alleviation measures is always a highly sensitive issue. It can damage the fragile social fabric and may result in greater poverty for some while favouring others. Such a risk may be avoided through a participatory approach which actively involves the poor and assists them in their efforts to gain control over their lives.

Disabled people are more likely to be poorer than their non-disabled peers because of the discrimination which accompanies disability, not because of the impairment itself.

They suffer from social exclusion and frequently find themselves trapped in a web of neglect. The problem is even more acute for disabled women, who encounter enormous prejudices and obstacles in their quest to participate in social and economic life.

A more enlightened society will seek to integrate disabled people, to give them opportunities to learn and to work as others do. It will adjust the physical environment to accommodate their special needs.

This planet belongs to all people. If some people are trapped somewhere, we must all come forward to remove the causes of their discomfort. At the same time we must leave our shores open for anybody who decides to join us, or any body who decides to part our company.

Poverty denies a person control over his destiny. Poverty means not being able to tell what tomorrow would be like. If we examine the situation carefully we will see that the poverty is neither created by the poor, nor sustained by the poor. It is the system of policies and institutions that we have built around us that creates and sustains poverty. Poverty is the denial of human rights. Over one billion people live below the absolute poverty line right now on this planet, are denied of almost all human rights. There is no way one can defend the existence of poverty anywhere. Poverty is a disgrace for the entire mankind. Because we allow another human being to die of hunger, or malnutrition, or common curable diseases, or exposure to climate, we are reduced to less human beings. If a particular world system is responsible for creating this massive poverty we must act to replace it.

Resource-wise or technology-wise, there is no reason why poverty should exist and continue to deepen and widen. If we make up our minds to wipe out poverty from the surface of the earth, the worst aspect of poverty can be removed within the next couple of decades.

Each human being is a wonderful creation of the creator. Each humanbeing is born with great potentials.

Poverty denies any opportunity for a person to achieve any of his/her potential. We have built a world system which is in the habit of pushing people down not building them up. It creates barriers around individuals, rather than remove them.

The most effective step that we must take to remove poverty is to create a system which creates enabling conditions for people and removes the existing barriers. The institutional barriers were skillfully crafted over the centuries to benefit a handful of people.

Resource-poor nations with high incidence of poverty waste away enormous human capability each day by denying poor people the use of their energy and ingenuity. If they could have been made economically active, not only they could have contributed in the national production, they would have helped expand the domestic market for the products produced. The disabled one can be transformed into the engine of growth if we only allow them to unleash their capacity.

We cannot be at peace with ourselves if we know there is a human being who lives a life worse than an animal. A human being is supposed to live differently than an animal. He /she is supposed to live a life with human dignity. Human dignity is what distinguishes a human being from an animal. When we cannot ensure this dignity for others, our own dignity becomes an empty pretense.

There must be a thousand and one ways to remove poverty from the earth. We may or may not know some of those ways already. Obviously there are many more ways yet to be designed, each more effectively than others. When we shall find them, howmany of them we shall find, how quickly we find them, will depend on how eager we are to find them. But to say that poverty cannot be overcome, directly and quickly, is to underestimate the capacity of human mind.

10

Towards a New Policy on Poverty Reduction

In recent years, the call for the policy which enables the reduction of mass poverty in India has increased not only from scientific point of view, but also from political and practical standpoint. Mass poverty is a problem crucial not only for the people concerned, but also for the future of humanity as a whole, and one that cries out for rapid solution. Indians still have not succeeded in permanently improving the living conditions of big parts of their population. Measures in terms of economic growth expected by Indians over the past fifty years, the preliminary growth-oriented development strategies pursued hitherto have not been unsuccessful. Many poor population groups continue to be excluded from the economic growth. The "Trickle-down effect" has failed and still fails to reach them.

Marginalization

As a result, the course development took in India led to the marginalization of broad sections of the population. Marginal groups arose that were denied access to the development process. They are characterized by a lack of active participation (exclusion from decision-making processes) and passive participation (failure to receive goods, services and social services). Such groups found themselves in a vicious circle. Because of their marginality they achieved only low rates of labour productivity and remained poor. They consequently slipped further towards the fringe of development. The greater the progress attained by the other sectors of the economy, the more acute the marginalization process became. The numerical increase in membership of these marginal groups was so great that in course of time they came to constitute a considerable proportion of the population.

This mass poverty is unacceptable not only from a humanitarian point of view. It also engenders problems of global dimensions. The increasing threat to the environment, a population growth stretching the capacity of the earth to its very limits, dramatic difficulties in India safeguarding food supplies, and the still unresolved debt crisis are only the tip of an iceberg that is to a large extent spawned and nurtured by mass poverty.

In view of this situation it seems paradoxical that the scientific literature related to the problem of mass poverty apparently finds it difficul to precisely define poverty, to ascertain its causes and to asses it in ethical, political, social and economic terms. The literature often states that there is neither a generally acceptable definition nor a more or less comprehensive and stringent theory of poverty. However, the lack of generally binding definitions of the concept is due not to the often cited difficulty of measuring the societal "quality" of poverty in quantitative terms. The reason is rather that both societies as a whole and individual social groups with differing values, religious convictions, ideologies and the resulting structures and functions, reach differing conclusions on where the line between "poor " and "not poor" is to be drawn. Views differ just as widely on the societal and individual salience of poverty. A generally valid concept of poverty applicable to every social context is accordingly not available.

Absolute and Relative Poverty

In discussing the problem of poverty, a distinction must be drawn between absolute and relative poverty. In the case of absolute poverty the insufficiency of resources available to an economic entity for the maintenance of physical subsitence is so drastic that the affected parties are no longer able to live in a manner "fit for human beings". In the case of relative poverty an economic entity has insufficient resources in comparison to other economic entities. This relative poverty does not necessarily mean that those affected are unable to live a life fit for human beings. It means merely that, due to the distributional structures prevailing in an economy, individual economic entities suffer deprivation to an unacceptable degree.

Poverty can be defined in both its aspects as deprivation. The deprivation can refer to various economic, social and/or political areas of human life. Poverty then means that various economic, social, and/or political needs of certain social groups are not satisfied, or are only inadequately satisfied. How drastic deprivation must be in individual cases and in what areas it has to occur before one can speak of absolute or relative poverty depends both on the observer's concept of tolerance and standards and on the given frame of reference.

The attempt to formulate an objective and generally valid definition of poverty must be abandoned. Poverty is a complex and multifaceted problem. Since it can be caused by deprivation in different areas, there are in reality different poverty profiles. The poor are, in fact, by no means a homogenous group. There is a multitude of different poverty groups with different interest and needs, such as women and children, the rural and the urban poor, members of various ethnic groups and religious communities. This can lead not only to conflict between poverty groups but also to discord within the respective groups, hampering the formulation of consistent strategies for reducing poverty.

Varieties of Poverty

If mass poverty is to be lastingly eliminated, its causes must be recognized and purposively eradicated. This is the only way to go beyond cosmetic treatment of the symptoms to provide permanent solutions. Poverty cannot be attributed to a single cause. It can always be traced back to the aggregation of various factors deriving to a large extent from the social system concerned. The diverse contexts in which the production factors labour, capital, and natural resources, technical knowledge, and the total environment relevant to development interact give birth to different "varieties of poverty". Successful projects and programmes for reducing poverty therefore require the fullest possible analysis of all the relevant elements and relationships of the concrete social system.

Other things being equal, the lower the per capita income of the population, the greater the extend of absolute poverty. Since this average income is in turn an indicator for the level of economic development, poverty can partially be explained in terms of the factors responsible for the economic underdevelopment of India. All strategies that contribute to improving the level of economic development can accordingly also provide an at least partial solution to the problem of poverty. In other words, a well conceived development policy can at the same time be a functioning policy for reducing mass poverty as well.

Growth with Poverty

On the other side it has to be seen that economic growth is not automatically linked with poverty reduction. Historical examples of the last three decades clearly show that economic growth can go hand in hand with poverty increase. Even in cases where the above mentioned requirements of a development-promoting policy have been fulfilled, growth was accompanied by an increase of poverty due to a missing participation of broad segments of the population in this growth process. Or to formulate it more generally: Between growth and distributional justice—defined at leas as reduction of mass poverty—can be a target conflict which has to be solved by other measures than by additional growth policies. In fact, the more unequally income is distributed, the more probable material poverty becomes. The factors determining the interpersonal distribution structure of a country thus also contribute to explaining poverty.

For the mass of the poor, ownership of productive resources is usually limited to their own (mostly unskilled) labour. To a lesser extent they may also have property rights in land (e.g., in the case of very small scale farmers), and in material assets (e.g., simple implements). The level of education and training that determines human capital is, by contrast, usually so low that no market improvements of their position can be expected. In most cases the poor of a society are also completely inadequately trained. With the exception of their labour, they thus dispose of no or of only very few productively utilizable resources. This is true for both the rural and the urban poor.

Their situation is made even more difficult by the fact that their resources can frequently not be used for farming or certain activities to be carried on despite adequate qualification, this can contribute just as much to poverty as repressive measures taken by big land owners against small farmers, or the activities of criminal groups in poor urban areas. The utilization of property rights can also be prevented by the complete absence of the additional resources (such as credits or jobs) required to carry on productive activities, or by their being available only on unacceptable conditions.

But even if the productively utilizable resources can actually be brought into use to produce goods and services, it is still not certain that an adequate level of income will be generated. At both the national and the international level, free entry to the market for the goods and services produced is not always attained, since there are frequent legal, physical, and psychological barriers to entering the market. In some cases, certain groups are not permitted to sell in institutionally secured markets, or may do so only subject to severe restrictions in the national context, for example, ethnic minorities, adherents of certain religions, members of particular castes.

Without a doubt, the behaviour of individual groups and persons contributes to breeding or consolidating their own poverty. A decisive role is played by the relation between the culture-specific willingness to achieve, personal attitudes towards achievement and actual capacity for performance—always with reference to underlying components of poverty. However, the social systems concerned are likely to be of far greater significance in generating poverty. As a rule, the poor are a marginal group within a social system who do not participate in the political, social and economic decision-making and development processes. This marginality is not an isolated phenomenon. It is system-related and often the very rational reaction of the poor to discriminating framework conditions for their economic as well as non-economic behaviour. If the poor are not permanently to remain passive recipients of the alms of material aid, the marginalized population groups must integrated into the system. For this purpose, considerable structural and functional changes in the systems concerned are necessary, including a certain degree of redistribution of resources, of economic opportunities, and of political power in favour of the poor. The precondition for such changes is that the ruling elites realize that in the long run mass poverty must almost inevitably lead to revolution which in most cases generates dramatic losses also for the elites themselves.

The Poor Must Act

However, in India there is no or very little ability and willingness on the part of the socially dominant groups to carry out such changes to the system. Since for the foreseeable future the poor can expect no real support from the system that discriminates against them, the initiative for such changes—if one excludes the possibility of external intervention—must come from the poor themselves. They must learn to help themselves. Self-help is consequently a constituent element in poverty-oriented development strategies. Self-help measures of this sort should aim not only to improve the situation of the poor as such. They should also contribute to overall development by personal initiative. An awareness of making a real productive contribution to a society is an important factor in 'socio-psychological' demarginalization. Such efforts at self-help should ideally develop within the group of the poor. Under the conditions prevailing in India, self-help must always be regarded as a group phenomenon and framed accordingly. Group successes generally provide the basis on which individuals gain greater opportunities to help themselves. If, however, the poor are unable to improve their situation by their own efforts, support for these efforts must be forthcoming. Such self-help support measures can be the object of a poverty-oriented development policy. They should most usefully not intervene at the level of the target group itself but—indirectly—at that of self-help support institutions, so as to avoid stifling burgeoning self-initiative efforts.

Every form of community self-help requires the participation of its members. Participation is thus not only a development instrument, but also a goal in itself, since it gives people a sense of self-respect and belongingness. It should thus be an essential component in any development strategy for reducing poverty. In contradiction to this demand, the poor are frequently treated more as objects than as subjects in the development process. The consequent lack of participation in the decision-making process can even be categorized as a primary cause of poverty. Indeed, as long as there is no genuine delegation of initiative, decision making and implementation, democratization will be no more than a slogan. If development is to be durable, it is essential to involve the marginalized groups in the planning and implementation of development programmes, and to give them a right of co-determination. This participation requires the poor to develop a critical awareness of their situation. They must stop accepting their poverty as more or less inevitable and adapting their behaviour to the situation. They must become conscious of their poverty and learn to regard it as deprivation. This critical awareness is the essential precondition for them being able to help themselves. Self-help and participation are thus inseparably interlinked.

Anti-poverty strategies directly addressing the target groups of the poor and which place no great value on self-help are doomed to failure in the long run. In the euphoric development policy conviction that help for self-help was the right way, it was, however, frequently overlooked that genuine self-help can only develop durably under certain minimum political, socio-cultural, institutional, and economic conditions. If such "margins for action" do not exist, the spontaneous development of self-help rapidly falls victim to the pressure of vested interests.

Gradual Approach Needed

What goals a poverty-oriented development policy would have to adopt, what strategies in reducing poverty ought to be developed, or what strategies can be successful in given contexts all depend on the concrete form taken by the circumstances as has been addressed here. At any rate, modesty is called for in this respect. However, ambitious it may sound to attempt to formulate a comprehensive policy for reducing poverty, in reality a gradual approach is to be recommended. In most cases it is expedient to restrict initial efforts to reducing material poverty, especially since theoretical knowledge has made most progress in this field.

It should always be kept in mind that anti-poverty strategies have political implications, since in essence they always amount to the redistribution of resources and political power, and the reorganization of institutions. The less evident the impression of a "zero-sum game", the greater will be the chances of prevailing an evolutionary development vis a vis the dominant society. From this point of view, poverty-oriented development policy is always a strategy of limited conflict, and is thus always caught between the desired evolution and the risk of revolution deteriorating into chaos that seldom improves the lot of the "poorest of the poor".

11

Women and Poverty

It is becoming more evident that the majority of the poor in developed and developing worlds are women. Poverty among rural women is growing faster than among rural men. Over the past 20 years, for example, the number of women in absolute poverty rose by 50 per cent as against some 30 per cent for rural men. The alarming evidence concerning the underlying trends for this process strongly indicates that the gender composition of the poor is veering towards a greater share of women.

Poverty manifests itself in many ways among migrant and refugee women, elderly women and children and indigenous women. Poverty is a complex, diverse and dynamic condition stemming out of depravation with respect to income, from social inferiority, isolation, physical weakness, powerlessness and humiliation.

Analysis of women's poverty suggest that its main causes stem from the perpetual disadvantage of women in terms of their position in the labour market, access to productive resources and income for the satisfaction of their basic needs. They also demonstrate that poor women possess exceptional resourcefulness, initiative and entrepreneurial spirit and that they show tenacity and self-sacrifice in trying to take a long-term view of their poor economic conditions and in safeguarding their livelihoods.

Development is the most important challenges facing the human race. The lack of progress in the last twenty years in the eradication of poverty and growing proportion of women among the poor is the single most important threat to the progress of development and its sustainability. As long as three-quarters of the world population continue to suffer from acute depravation, as long as profound imbalances in global consumption continue to persist, and more important, as long as the spread of poverty, particularly among women, continues unchecked, there can be no development. The history of the development process shows again that the economic status of women is the key variable in the solution to the poverty crisis. It is time for the full recognition of the fact that women are part of the solution to poverty and to the stagnating development, not part of the problem.

The Earth Summit in Rio, the Human Rights Conference in Vienna, the population Conference in Cairo and the Beijing conference all were milestone events in terms of advancing our understanding of the crucial role of women in development and focusing the attention of the international community on the issues concerning the role of women in the work place and in society. All of them drew attention to women's full and effective participation in development. None, however, full articulated how to achieve this challenging task.

It is important to retain focus on the issue of economic potential when discussing poverty among women because it is clear that power is only meaning something in practical terms if it is reinforced by economic power. Women have the means to transform productive resources into such power if only enabling environment is created. It is not the lack of capabilities, but that of resources which is clearly responsible for women's poverty.

Sometimes the so badly needed resources are not even truly scarce. Billions have been wasted on arms purchases around the globe and particularly in the countries which can not afford such misallocation of public funds. At the same time, women's organizations from grassroots to the international level are poorly funded. Such misallocation of resources at the time when poverty among women is increasing, is immoral and unacceptable, not only on the part of the governments which pursue such wasteful policies, but also on the part of the suppliers, who in most cases are developed economies.

Government's responsibilities do not end here. It is extremely important, and indeed it is the main duty of every government around the world, to provide a conducive environment for economic growth and stability by pursuing responsible and sound macro-economic policies which will enable the economy to grow without marginalizing women. When inflation is rampant, when political climate is unstable, leading to conflicts and civil strife, little can be done for poverty alleviation.

12

Empowerment for Women? The Gap between Theory and Practice

Actually, the situation of women has changed completely in the last 30 years. At the beginning of the 1970s women were a blind spot in both development aid and the debate on it. The promotion of women is now established in all state institutions and non-governmental organisations (NGOs). Gender training is to sensitive development workers to take a gender specific approach in analysing development processes, carrying out statistical surveys, and planning and evaluating activities.

From Integration to Empowerment

Those women who is in the 1970s criticised development policy and its actors for being one-eyed must now see themselves as line-promoters and idea-providers. All the terms they used have been adopted in official usage. The image of the woman has changed from being a Cinderella-like, hard-done-by person, the poor soul, the victim, to a dynamic, reliable actor with apparently inexhaustible reserves of energy and creativity to bring to bear in a development process that has got stuck. The concept of empowerment has replaced the old "integration in development" approach in the promotion of women. And the women's approach (Gender and Development). This calls for the inclusion of men, taking a close look at the gender relationship and changing it into the long run.

All this undoubtedly progress which illuminates the blind spot. So is that enough to please women critics of the male-dominated development aid scene and female lobbyists for the promotion of women? Have they achieved what they wanted? That is, a policy on women which on the one hand takes up their practical, everyday needs, but on the other works strategically towards eliminating the hierarchy between the genders by structural changes? The fact is that one must differentiate between what governments, multilateral institutions and NGOs are saying and what they are doing.

Redistribution of Social Power and Control of Resources

The empowerment concept makes clear the political and economic gap between men and women, it aims at a redistribution of social power and control of resources in favour of women based on a development strategy which is no longer oriented on growth, the world market and military power.

The concept has had seemingly record acceptance in the executive suites and programmes of the governments while at the same time its substance has been drastically diluted. Taken on board hook-line-and-sinker by official policy, its politically critical teeth-namely posing the power question—have been extracted. It now has no bite critical of development and social policy. It just stands modestly and harmlessly for every strengthening and participation of women.

Professionalization on the NGOs side and state orientation on the grass roots have brought activities nearer to one another. The modes of expression are identical. But where are women really at the centre of development practice? And where are they at the centre of developmental organizations? The promotion of women is still an appendage to development policy, including in most NGOs. That is shown not only by the low number of "pure" women's projects, but also by the subordinate role of women's interests and measures for women in integrated programmes. Defined as a "cross-sectional task", the advancement of women is often reduced to the mere addition of a women competent. For example, in the form of small-scale loans for sewing machines. The few women in the organizations are assigned a low-ranking and sparsely-equipped niche.

Lack of Long-term Strategy

The gender approach has made the yawning gap between rhetoric and practice even bigger. It might be useful as an instrument of analysis, if it is not debased to a technocratic checklist. But non-one at present knows for sure how it can be implemented. The international trend is to implement promotion of women less in "pure" women's projects than to integrate it in other activities. Parallel to that, there are signs of a trend in which the women's or gender sections of development agencies are being disbanded and integrated in country or specialist sections.

Currently, however, there is apparently still a lack of concepts for implementing a strategically oriented advancement of women. If integration, or "mainstreaming", now takes place at the various levels, it is to be feared that the promotion of women will peter out rather than spread.

At the same time, disenchantment prevails among those who have understood that the advancement of women is a means to more rights and opportunities in life, more self-confidence and social recognition. The demand to effect structural change through projects founders on the general conditions. Like development assistance as a whole, raising the status of women is also in many regions becoming increasingly merely disaster relief and survival aid. All involved have long known there are no universally applicable formulas for projects, and still, fewer handy "directions for use" for getting out of poverty and blasting open patriarchal suppression.

The dilemma is clear. The economic crisis, the over-indebted and socially inactive governments, and the men who steal away from responsibility are saddling women with ever increasing burdens in securing survival. Thereby the women urgently need support. At the same time, the limited impacts of promotional measures, or even their boomerang effect, and becoming more obvious.

Many women are being catapulted into the exploitation mechanisms of the market and money economy only when they get involved in projects. Or, at least, the projects are speeding that process. Because of the projects the women neglect subsistence production and their traditional principles of the moral economy. But it is also clear that as a result of training programmes, new forms of organization, development of new fields of action, and mobility, women's groups would collapse.

Thus, the old dilemma—of here a policy of small steps necessary for survival, and there big strategic and structural concepts—has got worse. But there's no way around it: the advancement of women must continue to seek bridges between being content with little and the vision of a development that is more just to women.

13

Women in Politics: Breaking Through the Barriers

The Participation of Women in Political life is today on the agendas of most political parties in India. However, attempts to translate this goal into concrete reality have had limited success. A basic reason for this is the lack of conceptual clarity about the genuine commitment to the issue. For any such endeavour to be successful, it must be recognised that the equal participation of women and men in decision-making in all spheres is a prerequisite for effective democracy.

Participation means more than female membership in political parties, female voter turnout in elections or a token female presence in political bodies. Participation must be meaningful and effective, and must include representation in the political arena. This includes not only formal or higher level decision-making forums, but also other political units: the family, community groups, associations, trade unions and local bodies. These are crucial areas for intervention within which women can easily understand the issues and play an effective role.

The identification of barriers to women's political participation is obviously a prerequisite for overcoming them, but the visible barriers do not necessarily reflect the entire situation, and are often merely indicative of more deep-rooted problems. Governments tend to address the issue by devising measures capable of showing quick results. But tackling visible barriers without addressing their root causes results at best in temporary success.

Overcoming the barriers means not only eliminating them but also ensuring women's participation through other means. Affirmative action measures should not be perceived as privileges or concessions, but as interim measures to reverse existing imbalances, until such time as genuine equality and parity is achieved.

India must review its policies, constitution and legislation to see whether these have been discriminatory towards women, or have been ineffective in promoting women's rights. Since the issue of women's participation cannot be addressed in isolation, one must identify and assess factors affecting the development of a democratic culture or the recognition of human rights concerns. These factors include the country's political history, its socio-cultural, ethnic and religious diversity, the impact of traditional, customary, feudal and tribal laws, and the use of religious interpretations regarding women's rights.

One must review the prevalent general situation of women. While inequalities and imbalances exist in all places some have stronger patriarchal structures wherein gender roles are more rigidly assigned. It is particularly important to assess women's political participation, including political rights, participation in election process and political parties, representation in legislative bodies and local councils, women in the civil service and in trade unions, and women's groups and lobbies.

Barriers to women's political participation can be legal, social, financial or political. In additions to identifying such barriers, it is useful to assess initiatives taken by governments and non-governmental organisations (NGOs), to evaluate successes and failures, identify the reasons and make modifications.

Based on the above, appropriate multi-pronged strategies and actions must be devised. It is important to develop a clear policy articulating the effective involving of women in the formulation of laws and policies which govern their lives.

Measures must be taken to ensure the principle of equality as a fundamental right. National legislation must be amended or repealed to remove any discriminatory provision. Positive legislation must be introduced to promote or protect affirmative action measures. The language of the law must clearly address itself to men and women, changing the practice of using the legal 'he' to include 'she'.

Research must be undertaken to cover information gaps. Monitoring mechanisms, guidelines and indicators must be devised and a process of periodic data collection established, to assess changing trends. Documentation and analysis of innovative initiatives must be ongoing, to help in devising and modifying strategies.

Women's human rights and power sharing issues must be integrated in all training progrmmes of government, semi-government and autonomous institutions. Key personnel involved in decision-making and implementation need to be made sensitive to gender issues. Political education and training programmes for women are needed at the community level, for NGOs and community-based organisations, communicators, development workers and media personnel, etc.

Campaigns to change attitudes and social norms and project a positive image of women can be run through educational efforts and the media, and public discussions and debates. A clear stand should be taken against any misrepresentation of religions which stands in the way of women's equality and political participation.

Workshops and seminars should promote closer interaction between women in NGOs, advocacy and research groups, government departments, political leadership, trade unions, worker's associations and the media.

A minimum quota should be established for women in all sectors and grades of the civil service, including government, semi-government and autonomous originations. A minimum percentage of key advisory positions, directorships, etc., should be reserved for women. Advertisements for government jobs should specifically state women's eligibility.

Electoral rolls should be systematically updated to include all eligible women. Education should be provided on electoral rights, political parties, election issues and concrete ways of holding candidates and political parties accountable. Political parties should publish their positions on women's rights issues, and encourage women to vote on issues that concern them. Constitutions of political parties should exclude provisions which condone or justify discrimination.

An adequate minimum representation of women in legislative bodies and local councils can be ensured by reserving seats through such means as putting women's names in priority positions on lists, providing financial support to female candidates, and making legal provisions that only those parties which give certain minimum number of tickets to women are eligible to contest elections.

A government ministry with the requisite authority should be designated as a focal point for devising policy, ensuring implementation and coordinating with other ministries and agencies.

An autonomous Permanent Commission on the status of women should be set up to function as a thinktank on women's issues, to commission policy research and to review, recommend and monitor the implementation of policies and Programmes in the field of development, rights and political participation. The Commission should comprise government representatives, NOGs, human rights organisations and experts in different areas.

A judicial authority should expedite women's human rights cases; this could take the form of a human rights bench, a tribunal or an equality ombudsman. These are only some of the basic principles and guidelines that can be adopted. Ultimately, however, no strategy can be effective unless it is also backed by the requisite political will and impetus.

14

Women in Authority : The Ideal and the Reality

At the current rate of progress it will take a very long time to bring about equality in sharing decision making between men and women in all areas. In terms of human rights and social justice, such equality is absolutely vital; it is also the best way to promote change with a human face. Would the world be better place if women had equal access to management positions.

A Near Absence

Almost everywhere in the world, women have the vote and account for over half of the electrorate. With but rare exceptions, however, their political activities are restricted to anonymous and informal roles in local communities. They hover at the margins of the higher levels of trade union, political, governmental and corporate life, and of interest groups. Until 1987, women occupied harely 10 per cent of parliamentary seats. They same holds true for the trade unions, despite the fact that women account for nearly one-third of union memberships Indeed, the women to have reached the leadership of a trade union can be counted on the fingers of one hand. This pattern of inequality is mirrored, indeed accentuated, in the employers' organizations, where women are practically absent. Everyone knows the situation in professional employment. Women continue to be concentrated in lower-qualified, lower-paid jobs, and very few manage to attain managerial posts, though the trend is on the increase.

Lower-paid Jobs

The "invisibility" of women in public life, and consequently in political, economic and professional activity, is both the cause and consequence of their being consistently barred from positions of authority. The way in which cultural and social models repeat themselves creates a setting that is hardly conducive to women progressing much beyond the limits of their homes and immediate working and living environment. Enmeshed in a tangle of little encouragement and probable reprobation, women are hesitant about struggling to advance in professional or political careers, as to do so would frequently put at stake the subordinate role that hitherto atleast guaranteed them a secure position within the family circle. On the other hand, as they hardly manage to participate fully in the decisions affecting their lives and families, it will prove difficult for them to break out of the vicious circle.

Rights and Obstacles

Why is it then essential for women to play an equal role in decision-making? One can approach this objective from three points of views. First, it is a clear question of human rights: women make up half the population and more than one-third of the workforce and so their right to full citizenship and equality of opportunity and treatment in employment must be clearly expressed by their participating in all levels of activity. Secondly, it is a matter of social justice to combat discrimination against women which is at its very harshest when it comes to employment. Thirdly, it is an essential requirement for the acceleration and effectiveness of development, as women are capable of providing a different sort of ability and creativity, which has not so far been tapped, and they can ensure a better balance in the allocation of resources and distribution of the benefits of progress.

Two Types of Obstacle

There are two types of obstacle to be overcome in order that women can have access to decision-making positions structural and situational. This includes the famous differences in levels of education, occupational experience and income levels as compared to men. These combine with and are reinforced by the situational factors such as the burden of family responsibilities, legal, psychological and material dependence on their spouses and male relatives, colleagues or bosses, and the fact that society is not prepared to change its attitudes and support women in assuming positions of responsibility. The deeply rooted "gender ideology" underlying all this constitutes a system of barriers to the upper echelons. It takes the form of values, attitudes and behavioural patterns which inhibit development and the recognition of the leadership qualities of women and which thus demand additional sacrifices from those who nevertheless strive to overcome them.

Additional Sacrifices

It has been estimated that women's participation in excess of 30 per cent in the upper echelons would be necessary for any noticeable difference to be made to the nature and tenor of the decisions taken in the areas affected. So what would this difference be? Women tend to speak with a "different voice" which as a rule lays stress on the social ethos of development, that is to say education, health, children, environment, dialogue and peace. Conversely, men tend to concentrate on the economic aspects such as production, trade, profitability, finance, technology and national defence. If we really aspire to any development of the human lot involving both economic growth and social equity, the best way to achieve this coveted objective will be by having men and women sharing in decisiontaking.

15

Promotion of Women

Women made up more than half the world's population, produced 80 per cent of its food, laboured for two-thirds of its working hours, were paid 10 per cent of its income and owned one per cent of its property.

These figures conceal manifold forms of the disadvantaging and discrimination of women. Such as the unjust division of burdens in families, the economic exploitation of women, the loss of their control over resources, and finally the unequal rating of paid and unpaid work. The latter, in the form of work for the family, on the land, for the community towards improving local living conditions, and nursing the old and the sick, adds up mostly to a 14 to 16 hour working day. True, employment of women has increased further everywhere in the world. But a number of them work in unsafe and socially unsecured conditions. They are also poorly paid and as a rule have hardly any chances to better themselves. Many women can earn money only in urban informal sectors or farming.

Global Public for Women

To be sure, the Decade of the woman (1976 to 1985), the adoption of the convention on eliminating every form of discrimination against women (1979), the key role of women in the development process and their rights have created a global public for them. Moreover, their activities have got underway a reorientation of international policies on women. But, despite numerous progressive international moves in the area of formal legislation, the political debates on the legal status of women are in no way over.

Making general statements on the correlation of the impacts of social development and the situation of women is difficult because the political, economic and cultural frame work conditions differ greatly from one country to another. However, discrimination against women manifests itself in most traditional as well as modern societies as a structural feature. Nowhere in the world are women treated "as good" as men, and all countries slip on the scale of human development when inequality between the sexes is measured. Differences between the life situations and opportunities of men and women still arise from unequal possibilities of access to employment, income, economic resources, health care, food, education and training.

Social development such as fundamental changes in traditional family and social structures, migration, urbanization, the contrast between traditional and "modern" ways of life, and often unfavourable economic developments for the majority of the people have a great influence on the role of the women in the various Third world countries. Moreover, the increasing differentiation of the South in terms of poorer and richer countries cannot obscure the fact that in the 1990s the general social conditions for the majority of women have not improved.

Almost one-third of all the people in the countries of the South live in life-threatening poverty, and the overwhelming majority of those are women. Female poverty has different aspects, such as poverty of income, low literacy, a lack of vocational training and the poverty of old age.

Further more, the continuing legal pluralism in many societies impedes efforts to achieve equality of status for women. Although in many countries men and women are meanwhile equal according to the constitution and legislation, there is still a great contradiction between constitutionally guaranteed rights and reality. According to religious law or custom, women in many countries are not equal to men. That means they have no property rights, or may not sign and contracts without their husbands' and constitutional rights, this implies the danger of becoming poor, particularly for single mothers, divorcees or widows.

Against this background it is no surprise that women are under-represented at political decision-taking levels, in government posts, political parties, trade unions and associations. The structures of many institutions give little support to women's interests, and managerial positions are held almost exclusively by men. In part, women-specific measures are seen as a compulsory exercise and, at best, tolerated as a fad.

New Opportunities

But in general the radical changes taking place in many countries open new opportunities for polices on women. On the one hand, this is because the extent of the disadvantaging and suppression of women is more visible. And on the other, because the fields of work for women have become wider—if mainly in urban centres. In some countries, women have been able to push through binding legal regulations (election laws, political party statutes, women's quota rules for local councils), in order to guarantee their stronger participation in parties and trade unions. With the programme slogans of "empowerment" and redistribution of power", women who are organized in self-help organizations, associations, networks and political parties are demanding participation in political decision processes and access to the political institutions. They are striving for social power in a bid to influence the factors which cause discrimination against them.

The transition from authoritarian to democratic forms of government in a great number of countries have placed women's organizations in a changed environment. There are now countless such bodies, and their combined clout is changing the status of women and helping to broaden their scope for social action. But in some countries women are still faced with considerable difficulties in organizing themselves with formal status.

On account of progressive impoverishment, however, the women's newly-won scope for action and shaping their lives is markedly cramped. Current developments such as religious fundamentalism or economic recession have inhibiting impacts on new approaches to policies on women in part, one must speak of a "backlash". Even where the legal position of women have been improved they have not been able to assert their social, economic and political rights. In some countries, it's feared that only elitist women's organisations will have a chance to break into the political process.

16

Lightening the Load for Women

Not only do women in India suffer greater poverty than men, they often have little choice but to pass it on to the next generation. Investing in women, therefore, is an effective way of building a better economic future for the poor.

Research findings from all sources are confirming what development practitioners have long observed: women are generally worse off economically than men, and the consequences of their poverty are more serious for future generations.

Women's poverty differs from that of men both in degree and in kind: women experience greater poverty and transmit their disadvantage more readily to their children, thus perpetuating the poverty cycle. At the same time, however, they are better able than men to protect children from the consequences of poverty.

It is this close connection between women's and children's fortunes that makes women's poverty a prime target for enlightened development practice. Anti-property policies need to reach poor women both to maximize social return on development investments and minimize the poverty of this and the next generation.

Breaking the Poverty Cycle

Poor women's rising participation in the world of paid work, however, does not necessarily guarantee a destiny of poverty. On the contaray, their earnings can protect children from poverty. Until fairly recently, the prevailing assumption was that any positive income effect of women's employment on children's health and well-being would be offset by negative effects of reduced child care time by working mothers or by the substitution of older sibling in child care. Recent studies, however, indicate a positive effect of women's employment on child health and nutrition. Women prefer to invest meagre earnings on child well-being and underscore the point that the income poor women earn can yield higher social benefits than income earned by men.

These positive effects of poor women's income-earning activities are not necessarily contradictory with the negative effects of women's increased work on their daughter's educational opportunities. It is likely that women need a minimum level of income to act on their preference to invest scarce resources on child-well-being, below which their additional work perpetuates rather than halts poverty.

Policy and Research Implications

It is therefore desirable to implement policies that reinforce the virtuous cycle between women's and children's well-being that can occur in poor families when women have more income, and avoid those that can instead trigger a vicious cycle of deprivation between mothers and children. Circumstances which increase poor women's unpaid or very low-paid work can foster the perpetuation of disadvantage. These include the effects of declining household incomes during economic downturns, the decrease in service provision by the State which accompanies Structural adjustment programmes, and many community and child-centered interventions that rely heavily on women's unpaid time. Anti-poverty packages need to reinforce poor women's roles as economic producers and avoid actions which increase women's unpaid labour for the promotion of family child welfare.

Projects which increase women's productivity in home and market production and expand their employment options can help to turn the vicious cycle of poverty into a virtuous one. This necessitates executing agencies which can work with women, and budget allocations to strengthen the capacity of institutions to implement and monitor gender-responsive employment programmes for the poor.

The reach of project interventions is restricted, however. Their impact is often short-lived and while they can help to contain the cycle of poverty between mothers and children, they cannot in themselves transform women's economic activities. Changes in the policy environment are required for the later. These include agricultural policies which target poor farmers and give women farmers access to land, credit and technical assistance; financial policies which promote the growth of small enterprises and foster entrepreneurship among women; and labour-intensive "pro-poor" economic growth policies. In addition, governments need to invest in upgrading women's occupational skills, and in a series of complementary measures, including overhauling social security systems, establishing gender friendly regulatory frameworks for agricultural and industrial growth, and legislate on child care options.

To guide these policies, we need: research that distinguishes families from households and seeks to understand the formation, structure and dynamics of families headed by women; longitudinal studies which provide a narrative for events in women's lives and assess the transmission of disadvantage between mothers and children; trend data which tracks changes in women's work as a result of changes in economic conditions and in implementation of economic and social policies; and analyses of the mechanics, costs and consequences of targeting interventions to female heads of households and poor women.

The policy-oriented research agenda is perhaps as ambitious as the policy agenda and both require funding. Investing in women should be an effective use of scarce development resources if these actions are guided by the basic principle of seeing women in India for what they are: economic and social agents and not merely passive recipients of welfare.

17

Equal Opportunities for Women in the Community

Over half the people in the Indian Community are Women. The change in women's contribution to society is one of the most striking phenomena of the late twentieth century. But although they have had the law behind them, women have yet to enjoy the equality they are entitled to in theory. Men need to contribute more to family life, while women have yet to make a real impact on decisions affecting the lives of everybody.

Technological advances have meant the decline of employment in manufacturing, and the growing dominance of service industries. This has meant more jobs for women, but not necessarily better working conditions. Most women are still in lower-paid jobs, and most still work mainly with other women in similar jobs and fields. Women are still under-represented in many sectors of industry, the professions and public service.

More and more women are involved in paid work. There is no job they cannot do, and they are entitled to equal pay for equal work, as well as the same terms and conditions at work, and the same opportunities for promotion. Giving women the opportunity to realize their potential in all spheres of society is increasingly important, for all only by involving both sexes to the full can we develop human resources on really democratic lines.

Equal Pay, Equal Opportunities

The right to equal pay for equal work without discrimination based on sex has to be set out. Equal treatment in access to employment, training, promotion and working conditions has to be encouraged. Equal treatment in social security, as well as for the self-employed are very much needed. Rights to maternity leave and pay, and a guarantee of adequate health and safety at work for pregnant women and nursing mothers are very urgent. The government has to encourage good practice on: Positive action, vocational training, childcare, combating unemployment, equal opportunities in schools, integrating women into working life, combating unwanted sexual behaviour at work, education, and updating protective legislation affecting women. There is still a great deal to be done before we can claim women in the community really get a fair deal and a chance to show what they can do.

Women are still often segregated into jobs that are less well-paid than those typically taken by men. They are often well qualified than men, and the jobs they do are often less secure. These are the kinds of inequalities the society must continue to combat and it will do so, as one of the ways of making sure women do not bear the brunt. Quality and quantity in women's employment is very important.

Better Opportunities to Earn a Living

Getting more women into paid work by promoting job opportunities, entrepreneurship and local employment should be the aim. The aim should be to help them fulfil their potential through better education, training and positive action. Upgrading their skills and equipping them with hi-tech know-how is a priority. Another major concern is helping parents juggle work and caring responsibilities via better services and terms of employment.

Getting Women in Positions of Power

It is hard to believe over half the Community's population is female, given how little direct influence women have over what happens in our society. In an electoral constituency where half the voters are women, and where concerns for education, family health and food are paramount, both contestants up for election are male, and they speak to a largely male audience. The women, who work long hours and worry and sacrifice for their families and homes, fuss with the tea, hush the children, over on the periphery. If they are there at all. Politics is 'men's business'.

Training to Keep up with the Times

Women need training if they are to benefit from growth and technological development. A network of training schemes, have to be set up to develop training for women, to publicize their needs, promote information exchanges and encourage the involvement of employers and trade unions.

Changing Minds in School

There is no job women cannot do. A working party is looking at ways of encouraging boys and girls to range more widely in the subjects they take in school. It should aim to support teachers trying to avoid reproducing anachronistic stereotypes.

Pregnant women, mothers of new-born babies and nursing mothers should have the peace of mind of knowing they have secure health and social rights. For women who already have to combine their professional life with running a home and looking after children, political activity requires considerable sacrifices. Women would be more ready to take them on if they thought they stood a chance of recognition on a par with men. That is far from being the case. If equal opportunities for women are provided definitely the country will develop at faster rate.

18

Fighting for Equality on all Fronts

In the wake of unemployment, global competition and deregulation, more and more women are joining an unforgiving job market. Are they in a position to exercise force against the discrimination they experience, and can they impose equality of opportunity? To change things, women need to enter into combat on several fronts.

"For a long time, companies considered publicity to be a luxury and, in difficult times, the 'advertising and communications' budget was always the first to be slashed. Today, employers have become more aware that publicity has become a trump card in their strategy. Why can't a similar awareness become possible on the subject of women's employment?"

Financial problems and an evolution of mentality are the two core themes discussed in this paper on the Equality of Women in the world of work.

A Dual Observation

It is of a two-fold general observation: women are more increasingly joining the ranks of the active population: however, this trend is not matched by a parallel improvement in the quality of jobs to which they have access.

It is foreseen that women's rate of participation will be close to that of men by the year 2000. In developing countries, the rate of women's activity is only 31 per cent on average, but this figure does not take into account the very large female participation in the informal sector and in agriculture. Thus, for example, in India, the adoption of a more general definition of "economic activity" pushed the participation of women from 13 to 88 per cent.

Women remained constrained in a relatively limited number of "feminine" sectors and occupations which are generally less well-paid and are less prestigious. During the last decade, however, an upward trend has emerged and more women are acceding to management and administrative posts and to specialized and technical professions. Moreover, an increasing number of women are setting up their own businesses. It can be noted, nonetheless, that very few salaried women are able to reach the higher echelons of responsibility due to the well-known "glass ceiling".

Among other disturbing observations is the increase in part-time work, which is especially prevalent among women with young children; other types of a typical work include temporary and occasional jobs, homework and subcontracting. Part-time workers are often young women who are less educated and less qualified than the average, which makes them more vulnerable. In Africa, in Asia and in Latin America, women are being called upon more and more to find work in the informal sector.

Even though some progress has been made in the area of wages, women's salaries are still between one-half and 80 per cent of those earned by men. Women's work is underestimated in most of the societies, and their income does not match their contribution to the economy. The difference in wages cannot be attributed to conditions of work alone. In the United States, in 1994 a woman in her twenties was likely to be earning 90 per cent of the rate of salary of her male counterpart.

Financial Problems

Financial problems and mentality issues emerged as two essential factors at every stage of the analysis of the causes of these persistent differences. The Fourm's participants' general consensus was that they should be tackled first of all.

Financial implications cannot be separated from the issue of women's employment, whether it is to justify its need or on the countrary to discourage it, or to explain the absence or lack of training of women who are available in the job market. Some example are:

— In the countries in transition in Central and Eastern Europe companies underpressure to increase profits do not want to maintain social support services, which earlier had backed women's participation in the active population. These pressures are compelling women to leave the job market as the cost of child care increases.

— In developing countries, especially in Asia, Africa and Latin America, the worsening of poverty and the increase in the number of single-parent families are requiring women to turn towards income-generating activities, but the lack of training and difficult access to credit constitute a major handicap.

— In Thailand, one of the major causes of young village girls resorting to prostitution is the state of poverty of their families, who are unable to afford secondary schooling for them.

Prejudices and Stereotypes

Several examples can also be found in the persisting traditions and stereotypes which are an obstacle in the path of women's march to equality of opportunity in the world of work.

— The Nordic countries, in particular Sweden, have instituted a parental leave which enables either one of the parents to take care of the young children at home; but it can be noted that very few fathers avail themselves of this opportunity.

— The status of a profession falls as the number of women entering it increases; salary levels thus become relatively less competitive. This trend is particularly clear in the teaching professions and in some medical professions.

— Measures of positive action are becoming more and more general. They cannot be successful unless they tackle discrimination on all fronts, together with the fixed ideas that are prevalent on the subject of the sexes. In fact, solutions to the financial problems that women's work causes are themselves going through an evolution in mentalities.

In a highly competitive job market, opportunities available to women are conditioned by the comparative cost of women's labour, as it is perceived by the employer. By virtue of the legislation in force in the majority of countries, the obligations linked to maternity protection and family responsibilities tend to increase the direct costs of women workers; generally, employers bridge this gap by lowering the wages of women or limiting recruitment to childless women. This form of discrimination can also go as far as requiring medical certificates to guarantee sterility.

A Global Programme

To avoid such tendencies, efforts should be channelled toward two fronts. First, evaluating the relationship between a real cost-benefit (including the criterion of effective productivity) with a view toward eliminating the false idea that women workers are more expensive.

Secondly, making sure that in legislation, in practice and especially in the mentality of men and women all around the reproductive function and care of persons are recognized as social functions whose costs should be footed by society as a whole.

Recognizing the universal nature of the problem and the various fronts where one would need to enter into combat, this programme should aim at changing the relationship of power between men and women. For this change to become permanent, it will be necessary to consolidate the ground gained as the process continues.

Remedies should be composed of measures touching upon, among other areas, legislation and its control, access to jobs, to training and to resources, the reconciling of professional activities with family responsibility, outreach measures to groups of underprivileged women, improvement of information and research, the participation of women in decision-making and the mobilization of public opinion.

19

Population Growth and Women's Role in India

We have limited economic resources. There is a pressing need to abolish poverty. If population grows unchecked, abolition of poverty becomes very_difficult. Due to the rise in population, illiteracy is growing as educational facilities are not expanding as fast as the population. Though employment facilities are being provided, we are not able to solve the unemployment problem. Though production and national income are rising, standard of living is not rising at the same rate. Thus growing population remains a serious draw back.

Conventional wisdom holds that slowing population growth is the key to solving a vast array of social, economic, and environmental problems. To be sure, in a world of finite resources, unlimited growth in the number of people requiring food, shelter, and work, not to mention access to natural resources, cannot be sustained. But the increasingly singular focus on demographics simply deflects attention from the fundamental social conditions—poverty, inequity, and the object status of women—of which population growth is not the cause, but the consequence.

In India, as in much of the world, women are last in line for education, job training, credit, and sometimes even food—despite the fact that raising the status of women is the most effective way both to reduce birth and to achieve higher standards of health and economic productivity.

In India's tradition-bound society, where child bearing is often the only route to status and security, the majority of women have little to gain from having fewer children. The government, by contrast, is bent on cutting birth rates in half over the next decade, but has shown little commitment to meeting women's needs. And so a vicious cycle is perpetuated. As long as the status of women remains low, voluntary family planning efforts will continue to founder, tempting the government to use pressure to meet its demographic goals.

India will surpass China as the world's most populous country by the middle of the next country, each day the number of people who lack access to adequate food, health care, housing, clean water, and education spirals upward.

Female Education

Female education is the single most; influential determinant of both lower birthrates and increasing empowerment for women.

Indian society manages to devote fewar resources to educating its girls than its boys. At the household level, cultural restrictions on female behaviour combined with the need for cheap household labour create a sharp gender gap in literacy. In both the Hindu and Muslim traditions, for example, nations of female "modesty" and "purity" dictate that unmarried females remain separate from unrelated males. Because the bulk of India's teachers are men, and most schools educate boys and girls under the same roof, many traditional families keep their daughters home, regardless of their income. Moreover, parents are apt to invest in educating girls only when they perceive that long-term gains will outweigh immediate costs.

For the impoverished majority, the expense of sending a girl to school–paying for uniforms, books, especially when young girls are required to work at home and in the fields.

Women's lack of knowledge translates directly into poor nutrition and health for themselves and their offspring. In turn, these conditions cause high infant mortality—for which many women compensate by having more babies.

Nutrition and Health

Nutritional and health status is also marked by gender disparity. Both boys and girls in India are nutritionally disadvantaged, as nearly half of the country's households fail to provide even the minimum daily caloric requirements. But malnutrition is far more prevalent among females than males. From birth, male children consistently receive more and better food than their sisters, even though the nutritional needs of prepubescent boys and girls are virtually identical. Boys, given the same level of illness, are taken to doctors more often than girls. As a result of this neglect, far more girls than boys die in the critical period between infancy and age five.

Discrimination in feeding and health care produces one of India's most provocative signs of gender bias: In fact, the ratio of women men in the country has been declining.

Women and Family Income

Son preference and the subsequently biased allocation of family resources is based on a serious of myths the Indian government has failed to combat. One is the notion—not peculiar to India—that females do not contribute to family income. Throughout the world, women bear the "invisible" burdens of unpaid domestic work and childbearing, the economic value of which is rarely reflected by official statistics.

Young girls in India generally work longer hours than boys of the same age. By age 10, girls in low income families are working eight or more hours a day assisting their mothers by tending siblings, collecting water and firewood, herding small animals, weeding fields, or facing the daily grind of low-paid child labour in the marketplace.

The poorer the family, the more vital the economic contribution that women and girls make, especially in the growing number of female-headed households.

Indifference Towards Women

The attempts to enhance agricultural productivity disproportionately benefit men.

Expansion of the irrigated area allocated to cash corps, such as groundnut and cotton, has come at the expense of food crops on which women depend to feed their families. And while the mechanization of plowing and leveling that comes with these projects reduces the traditional workload of men, that for women actually increases. Women still must carry out by hand the tasks of weeding, turning soil, and harvesting, but over much larger areas.

The result is to deepen women's poverty and enhance the perceived value of having many children to help with chores.

Not surprisingly, the share of married couples of reproductive age using contraceptives—now 40 per cent—is low, and most of these are holder couples who turned to sterilization (counted as a form of contraceptive) only after having large families.

This bleak situation is shadowed by an ominous fact of history. Past attempt to reduce births in the absence of social changes enhancing women's status have been accompanied by increases in violence against females—in the beating and abandonment of women who don't bear sons, in female infanticide and child neglect, and in the rising use of abortion for sex-selection.

Experience shows that even in India, with its immense tangle of troubles, well-designed programmes can produce dramatic improvements in family health while improving women's status and reducing births.

Increasing young girl's access to education and offering older women a chance for learning are essential to increasing female autonomy. Requisite steps include serious efforts to train and hire more female teachers, to set up literacy and tutoring campaigns in every state, and to encourage the growth of women's empowerment groups to foster changes at the village level. These strategies already have been proven in the southern state of Kerala, internationally lauded for its dramatic gains in the health and economic status of women and in slowing population growth.

Equally important are broad public education campaigns to raise awareness of the immense value of women's work and welfare to families and societies. The mass media also could be enlisted in the effort to change dramatically social perceptions of women's roles by depicting positive images of women and their economic contribution to society.

Much of the battle to win recognition of the importance of women's lives and health to societies will have to be fought by women themselves. Indications are that women are responding to the challenge.

By filling the existing demand for quality voluntary family planning services, the government can make cuts in birthrates of at least 25 per cent over the next decade, thereby starting the process toward reducing the country's population. Equally critical to a long term strategy of sustainable development is a sustained political commitment to improve the status of women throughout India. Only by working toward all of these objectives simultaneously can the dreams of women for full partnership in society come true.

20

Stop Child Labour

Although the internationally recommended minimum age for work is 15 years and the number of child workers under the age of 10 is far from negligible, almost all the data available on child labour concerns the 10 to 14 age group.

Traditionally, the proportion of working children has been much higher in rural than in urban areas—nine out of ten are engaged in agricultural or related activities. In the towns and cities of India where child labour has increased steadily as a result of the rapid urbanization of recent years, working children are found mainly in trade and services and to a lesser extent in the manufacturing section.

Available statistics suggest that more boys than girls work. It should be borne in mind, however, that the number of working girls is often under estimated by statistical surveys, as they usually do not take into account full-time housework performed by many children, the vast majority of whom are girls, in order to enable their parents to go to work.

Girls, moreover, tend to work longer hours, on average, than do boys. This is especially true for the many girls employed as domestic workers, a type of employment in which hours of work are typically extremely long. This is also the case of girls employed in other types of jobs who, in addition to their professional activity, must help with the housework in their parents' home.

One of the factors affecting the supply of child labour is the high cost, in real terms, of obtaining an education. Many children work to cover the costs of school expenses. But, many schools serving the poor are of such abysmal quality or chances of upward mobility for graduates are so slim, that the expected return is not equal to the sacrifice made... . While it is true that many children drop out of school because they have to work, it is equally true that many become so discouraged by school that they prefer to work.

In manufacturing industries, children are most likely to be employed when their labour is less expensive or less troublesome than that of adults, when other labour is scarce, and when they are considered irreplaceable by reason of their size of perceived dexterity.

Many working children face significant threats to their health and safety. The majority are involved in farming and are routinely exposed to harsh climate, sharpened tools, heavy loads as well, increasingly, as to toxic chemicals and motorized equipment. Others, particularly girls working as domestic servants away from their homes, are frequent victims of physical, mental and sexual abuses which can have devastating consequences on their health.

Prostitution is another type of activity in which children, especially girls, are increasingly found. The AIDS epidemic is a contributing factor to this trend, as adults see the use of children for sexual purposes as the best means of preventing infection. The laissez-faire attitude of the authorities incharge of national and international tourism is also largely responsible for the current situation.

Another extremely serious problem is child slavery in India. A large number of child slaves are to be found in agriculture, domestic help, the sex industry, the carpet and textile industries, quarrying and brickmaking." Child slavery predominates mainly where there are social systems based on the exploitation of poverty, such as debt bondage, when the motivation is the debt incurred by a family to meet a social of religious obligation or simply to acquire the means of survival.

There is a growing body of opinion that national and international efforts need to be more sharply focused on the most abusive and hazardous forms of child labour, granting them first concern and priority. Perhaps the most telling social argument against child labour is that its effects are highly discriminatory, adding to the burden and disadvantage of individuals and groups already among the socially excluded while benefiting those who are privileged. For that reason, child labour is inconsistent with democracy and social justice.

Action Required at the National Level

In the majority of states of India where child labour is common, the action taken until now to combat it has in no way been proportional to the extent and gravity of the problem. Many state governments have left it to economic growth and legislation alone to provide the solution. Experience has shown however that, unless specific measures are taken, growth in itself rarely benefits the very poor and that legislation means little where it is not vigorously enforced.

The problem of child labour will not be solved overnight. It is one of the many facets of poverty and underdevelopment. Resources available to reduce its extent and damaging effects are by definition scarcest in India that need them the most. Priorities must therefore be set.

No Effective Programme Without Hard Information Research

Almost everywhere, hard information is lacking on how many children are working, what they are doing, where and in what conditions. Without such data, it is virtually impossible to develop effective policies and programmes. Establishing, in some cases improving, data collection systems on child labour is an essential first step.

Raising Awareness

A common attitude toward child labour in India is to accept it as an unavoidable consequence of poverty. Given the low quality and implied cost of the education services available to the poor, many parents, having themselves worked as children, tend to consider an early entry into the labour market, rather than schooling, as the best way to equip their children with skills useful for their future as adults.

Another difficulty is inherent in the fact that children working in rural areas, in urban informal sector workshops or as domestic servants in private household are not readily visible. An effective effort to protect children from work place hazards or abuses must therefore, begin by making the invisible visible. Experience clearly shows that significant public pressure is required to make progress on the child labour issue politically possible. As long as the general public, and in particular the middle and higher classes, consider that child labour is part of the harsh reality that makes good economic sense, the conditions for change will not be met.

The Government of India has restricted its role to enacting legislation, but has been passive in its enforcement. Most initiatives against child labour have traditionally come from Non-Government Organizations. In spite of their dedication however, their resources cannot be equal to the magnitude of the task. All levels of society need to do their share.

Some types of action can be provide only by the Central Government: child labour legislation and attendant enforcement mechanisms, the setting of public policy priorities and a publicly-funded system of basic education that offers quality schooling for all, including the children of the poorest families.

Trade Unions Bring Abuses to Light

Trade unions, are the logical leaders for bringing child labour abuses to light. They are ideally placed to document concrete cases of abusive child labour and to monitor the effectiveness of legal instruments and the performance of the labour inspectorate in the child labour field.

Employers and their organizations also have good reasons to be interested in the issue. Besides obvious humanitarian and social reasons, combating child labour makes perfect sense on economic and business grounds. Emotionally or physically damaged children have little chance of becoming productive adults.

NGOs' Strength is with Children Already Working

Like trade unions, NGOs can help to discover and publicize specific cases of abusive child labour. They are, in addition especially good at devising and implementing action programmes on behalf of children already in the labour market. Close to the children, they generally enjoy the trust of the local communities concerned and are well placed to appeal to their hearts and resources.

The participation of other segments of civil society—The media, universities, parliamentarians, teachers and educators should be enlisted in the fight against child labour. All are valuable allies and can cooperate in complementary ways.

Establishing the Required Institutional Capacity

To formulate and execute a national plan of action against child labour, institutional mechanisms must be established or strengthened within the governmental apparatus. These can then be entrusted with the responsibility for setting priorities, coordinating the activities of the various ministries concerned, promoting private sector participation and for launching and supporting pilot schemes to find new ways of preventing child labour and of rehabilitating those who have been rescued from it.

Improving Legislation and Enforcement Measures

In India legislation exempts from coverage precisely the kinds of work in which children are most engaged (agriculture, family undertakings, small workshops, domestic service). A necessary first step to expanding protection under the law is to ensure that the main places where children work and the worst forms of child labour are encompassed by national legislation.

Improving Schooling for the Poor

The single most effective way to stem the flow of school-age children into abusive forms of employment or work is to extend and improve schooling so that it will attract and retain them. Recent trends however leave little room for optimism in that regard. In the eighties and early nineties resources devoted to education have dwindled steadily in India. The poor situation of the economy and the effects of structural adjustment policies were the reasons generally given for this decline.

Using Economic Incentives

As poor families need the income deriving from the employment of their children, it has often been considered appropriate to provide cash or in-kind payments as replacement.

Lively International Debate Over Negative Incentives

The advisability of using negative economic incentives has been the subject of much recent public debate. In Europe several department stores have decided not to sell products such as carpets unless they are certified to be made without child labour. Such movements by consumers and manufacturers alike have been accompanied by powerful efforts on the legislative and trade fronts as demonstrated by the hot debate on the incorporation of a social clause into international trade agreements. The United States has introduced conditionality into its Generalized System of Preferences, as has the European Union, to promote, among others, better labour standards and thereby discourage the use of child labour. A bill aiming at banning the import into the United States of goods produced by children (the Harkin Bill), has generated concern among employers and governments in countries heavily dependent on the United States for their exports.

There is no doubt that initiatives of this kind have helped significantly to raise public awareness about child labour. However, they have also had unintended consequences. The mere threat led employers of various industries to abruptly dismiss tens of thousands of children, the end result was that the dismissed children shifted to other occupations, which were often more hazardous than the jobs they used to perform in the previous industry, with no instances of children returning to school.

This example suggests that such measures may drive child labour into the less regulated domestic economic sectors. It also suggests the need to move children away from the work place in a phased and planned manner, instead of simply throwing them overnight, and unaided, into a far worse situation.

21

Child Labour—Targeting the Intolerable

We all know that child labour is one of the faces of poverty and that many efforts over many years will be required to eliminate it completely. But, there are some forms of child labour today which are intolerable by any standard. These deserve to be identified, exposed and eradicated without further delay.

The problem of child labour is so enormous and the need for action is urgent, choices must be made about where to concentrate available human and material resources. The most humane strategy must therefore be to focus scarce resources first on the most intolerable forms of child labour such as slavery, debt bondage, child prostitution, work in hazardous occupations and industries, and the very young, especially girls.

In addition, a comparative study carried out over a period of 17 years in India on both children who attend school and children who instead work in agriculture, industry or the service sector showed that working children grow up shorter and weigh less than school children.

In Bombay, the health of children working in hotels, restaurants, construction and elsewhere was found to be considerably inferior to that of a control group of non working school children. Working children exhibited symptoms of constant muscular, chest and abdominal pain, headaches, dizziness, respiratory infections, diarrhoea and worm infection.

Sexual Differences

Girls more often work in domestic labour, boys work in construction, fields and factories, leading to sexual differences in exposure to hazards. Girls, because of their employment in households, work longer hours than boys each day. This is one important reason why girls receive less schooling than boys. Girls are also more vulnerable than boys to sexual abuse and its consequences, such as social rejection, psychological trauma and unwanted motherhood. Boys, on the other hand, tend to suffer more injuries resulting from carrying weights too heavy for their age and stage of physical development. There are unsafe and abusive working situations for children. Some examples of these include:

- ***Slavery and Forced Child Labour***: Of all working children, those bound in slavery and forced child labour are the most imperiled. Children are still being sold outright for a sum of money. At other times, landlords buy child workers from their tenants, or labour "contractors" pay rural families in advance in order to take their children away to work in carpet-weaving, glass manufacturing or prostitution.

- ***Prostitution and Trafficking of Children***: The commercial sexual exploitation of children is on the rise, even though the subject has in recent years become as issue of global concern. Children are increasingly being bought and sold across national borders by organized net works.

- ***Agriculture***: Children work in agriculture throughout the world and often face hazards through exposure to biological and chemical agents. Children can be found mixing, loading and applying pesticides, fertilizers or herbicides, some of which are highly toxic and potentially carcinogenic. Pesticide exposure poses a considerably higher risk to children than to adults, and has been linked to an increased risk of cancer, neuropathy, neuro-behavioural effects and immune system abnormalities.

Mortality among child farm workers from pesticide poisoning is greater than from a combination of childhood diseases such as malaria, tetanus, diphtheria, polio and whooping cough. The operation of farm machinery by children also leads to many accidents which kill and maim.

- ***Mining***: Child labour is used in small-scale mines in many countries. Child miners work long hours without adequate protective equipment, clothing or training. They are also exposed to high humidity levels and extreme temperatures.

Mining hazards include exposure to harmful dusts, gases and fumes that cause respiratory diseases that can develop into silicosis, pulmonary fibrosis, asbestosis and emphysema after some years of exposure. Child miners also suffer from physical strain, fatigue and musculoskeletal disorders, as well as serious injuries from falling objects. Children working in gold mines are endangered by mercury poisoning.

- ***Ceramics and glass factory work***: Child labour in these industries is common. Children often must carry molten loads of glass dragged from tank furnaces at a temperature of 1500-1800 degrees Centigrade. They also work long hours in rooms with poor lighting and little or no ventilation. The temperature inside these factories, some of which operate only at night, ranges from 40 to 45 degrees Centigrade. Floors are covered with broken glass and in many cases electric wires are exposed. The noise level from glass-pressing machines can be as high as 100 decibels or more, causing hearing impairment.

The main hazards in this industry are exposure to high temperatures leading to heat stress, cataracts, burns and lacerations; injuries from broken glass and flying glass particles; hearing impairment from noise; eye injuries and eye strain from poor lighting; and exposure to silica dust, lead and toxic fumes such as carbon monoxide and sulphur dioxide.

- ***Matches and fireworks industry***: Match production normally takes place in small cottage units or in small-scale village factories where the risk of fire and explosion is present at all times. Children as young as three are reported to work in match factories in unventilated rooms where they are exposed to dust, fumes, vapours and airborne concentrations of hazardous substances—asbestos, potassium chlorate, antimony trisulphide, amorphous red phosphorous mixed wit sand or powdered glass and tetraphosphorous trisulphide. Intoxication and dermatitis from these substances are frequent.

- ***Deep-sea fishing***: In many Asian countries, children work in muro-ami fishing, which involves deep-sea diving without the use of protective equipment. The children beat on coral reefs to scare the fish into nets. Each fishing ship employs up to 300 boys between ages 10 and 15 recruited from poor neighbourhoods. Divers reset the nets several times a day, so that the children are often in the water for up to 12 hours. Dozens of children are killed or injured each year from drowning or from decompression sickness or fatal accidents from exposure to high atmospheric pressure predatory fish such as sharks, barracudas, needle-fish and poisonous sea snakes also attack the children.

- ***Child domestic workers***: Child domestic service is a widespread practice in many developing countries, with employers in cities often recruiting children from rural villages through family, friends and contacts. Violence and sexual abuse are among the most serious and frightening hazards facing children at work, specially those in domestic service. Such abuse leads to permanent psychological and emotional damage.

- ***Construction***: Children undertaking heavy work, carrying massive loads and maintaining awkward body positions for a long time can develop deformation of the spinal column. Sometimes, the pelvis can also be deformed because of excessive stress being placed on the bones before the epiphysis has fused. Children working in construction and other fields are exposed to other toxic and carcinogenic substances, including asbestos, one of the best known of human carcinogens.

One reason why modern societies and governments have not been more active in curbing the most harmful forms of child labour is that working children are often not readily visible. It is a matter of 'out and sight' out of mind'.

22

Child Labour in Weaving Industry

Approximately 1,30,000 children work in India's hand-knotted carpet industry. The working conditions are often poor, involving long hours sitting in one position, breathing cotton and wool fibres, eye-strain from doing very fine work and poor lighting. In the smallest enterprises the only light often available is the natural light filtering in through an open doorway.

Children are more likely to work in larger establishments: the smallest enterprises are family operations where the father and other family members might both weave carpets and till a plot of land, whereas the larger business use almost all hired labour. In the one-loom enterprises, approximately 14% of weavers are children, while the number of a child labourers rises to around 33% in businesses with five or more looms.

Although the proportion of child labour rises with the size of firm, the proportion doesnot rise as the quality of carpet increases; in fact, children are more likely to work on low-quality than on the highest-quality carpets. There is "no evidence that children dominate any particular design or quality niches". The opposite would be the case if the "nimble fingers" argument were true.

If the "nimble fingers" argument does not hold in the hand-knotted carpet industry, then it probably doesnot hold in other industries. Rejection of the "nimble fingers" argument is reinforced by the ability of adults to master carpet-weaving skills. Many adolescents and young adults who attend government training centres go on to run their own weaving businesses, while weavers say it takes a year to become fully proficient, whether one starts as an adult or a child.

Enterprises Often Small and Impoverished

The workforce of the hand-knotted carpet industry is mired in poverty. Most weaving enterprises in the Indian hand-knotted carpet industry are small, marginal operations run by poor and illiterate men, and they have no margin to pay higher wages. Most of the employers have never attended school, then began weaving before age 14. An enterprise normally consists of a loom set up in a family's one-room cottage, with perhaps an additional loom, or looms, in an attached veranda or a shed. Male family members, including children, provide the bulk of the labour.

India's Factories Act has influenced the current structure of the carpet industry. Costly health, safety and labour regulations to which large firms are subject do not apply to cottage industries. Only a small proportion of establishment have five or more looms.

Competition Limits Retail Price Increases

While child and adult weavers have similar productivity, there is a cost advantage to hiring child labour: children earn less while apprentices than do fully-trained weavers, and their addition to the workforce depresses the going wage rate. Replacing the 22% of children in the workforce would likely cause the wage bill to rise by about 5%.

Given the small scale of many weaving enterprises and the fact that weaving charges make up approximately 40% of the total production cost, with the loom owner receiving a fee equivalent an to 10% of production costs for supervision and provision of looms and premises, it is clear that the use of child labour can add greatly to the revenues and profits of loom owners.

The extra labour costs involved in eliminating child labour become much easier to absorb further down the distribution chain. Importing country wholesalers mark up the carpets around 65% while foreign retailers typically mark up the carpets by approximately 200%. With sales or value-added tax, the carpets can easily cost four times as much to the consumer as the Indian export price. This means that the overall savings in production costs from the use of child labour are very small when compared to the foreign retail price.

Finding solutions which satisfy both local weavers and foreign retailers must avoid a beggar-thy-neighbour spiral . If carpet producing countries simultaneously implemented a no-child-labour strategy in their hand-knotted carpet industries, none of them would be at a competitive disadvantage.

Methods of reducing child labour such as those used in the garment industry where there is tripartite collaboration to ensure that the children are treated well and that there are educational opportunities for them until they are replaced without economic hardship to their families, is not likely to work in the hand-knotted carpet industry. Neither labelling nor inspection is likely to work here because the industry is too fragmented. It is impossible to control the thousands of cottages where one or two carpets per year are woven. We need solutions that address the general problems of poverty while developing alternative sources of both employment and education.

Child labour is not necessary in the carpet industry. Children do not possess a unique skill and there is a ready pool of surplus adult labour ready to take over from them. "People should not be fooled into thinking that child labour is necessary for the industry to survive. The irreplaceable skills, or "nimble fingers" argument should no longer be used to justify the use of child labour in the carpet industry or any other industry".

23

The Indian Economy and the Cattle Wealth

Though most of the Indians are virtual vegetarians, India is home to more cattle than any other country. The country's bulging barnyard results from a complex equation of economic need and religious reverence for cows. The sum is that cattle have outstripped the resources available to feed them, and their overgrazing is racking up a sizable environmental bill. The pressure of too many cattle on too little land is turning India's beloved beast of burden into one of the country's worst environmental enemies. Many cattle exist on starvation rations, too emaciated to serve their vital roles as milk producers and draft animals. The health of Indian cattle mirrors the wealth of their owners. The stall-fed dairy herds that supply milk products to city residents are usually well-nourished, as are the draft animals of wealthier farmers. By contrast, the animals of the poor maraud through urban yards for garbage or forage any open rural land, since their owners lack both cash and land to feed them.

Hinduism has long been blamed for India's millions of hungry bovines. Under Hindu tradition, cows are revered, and laws forbid their slaughter in all but two states, Kerala and West Bengal. Recently, the leader of the Hindu Nationalist Party has even called for abolishing cow butchering by non-Hindus.

Though its contribution to India's herd size cannot be dismissed, Hinduism is much less a consideration than is the economic value of bovines to rural Indians. From the perspective of the poor, a cow is a blessing. Even a scrawny bull may be able to pull a plow—a much-needed service in India, where 70 per cent of farmland is still tilled by draft animals.

Cattle manure is invaluable for fertilizer, fuel, and building mud walls. For a rural woman, a cow or a goat may be the only property she ever owns. When an animal dies, its hide can be sold for leather, its skeleton for bone meal. A cow may not be the path to riches, but it is an added hope for survival.

In a country already crowded with huge population, though, space for India's millions of cattle has been steadily shrinking. Unable to divert precious cropland to fodder, poor hoarders instead run their beasts on the fallow lands of wealthier farmers and on common land, including village forests, wasteland, and roadsides. Grazable land, however, is disappearing. Land reforms have divided common areas among farmers, irrigation has turned dry rangeland to cropland, and tractors have plowed under fallow fields. Even forestry projects have usurped former grazing land for trees. All told, India's dry regions have lost more than one-third of their common land.

On the common lands that remain, traditional village management is crumbling under population and economic pressures, so grazing is uncontrolled. As cattle overgraze grasses, they clear the way for an invasion of weeds and woody shrubs, and topsoil becomes exposed to the erosive power of wind and rain. Parched subsoil and deep gullies are all that remain in many areas.

As the condition of common lands has deteriorated, the number of goats has surged. With less discriminating palates than cattle, goats eat the weeds and shrubs on degraded areas cattle ignore. India's forests, caught between fodder and fuelwood needs, have not escaped destruction. Though state forests are usually off-limits to villagers, poor women—who collect most fodder—are driven to graze their animals on woodland grasses and illicitly cut branches for fodder. Constantly pruned back, trees eventually die, and as the canopy opens and grasses vanish, soils dry up and erode. India's deforestation and erosion problem is largely a cattle feed problem.

Relief for India's hungry cattle and battered land is not likely soon, although the loss of common land has actually compelled some peasants to give up their animals. What appears the obvious solution—killing off "excess" cattle—is constrained by legal codes and, more importantly by poverty. Eliminating the scraggliest cattle, which belong to the poor, would make the people with the least suffer the most.

Poverty also has hampered the Government's strategy to boost each cow's productivity so that fewer are needed. For example, as part of a dairy development program dubbed Operation Flood, the Indian Government distributes European cow breeds and buffaloes that produce more milk. But villagers who can't afford low-cost fodder can hardly buy the expensive feed grains that the new animals require. On low-quality rations, the new breeds fare worse than their less-pedigreed cousins.

India's cattle will likely crowd fields and streets for years to come. There are no simple solutions, but without concerted efforts to meet the feed demands of these animals, the environmental destruction they cause may make India's favoured beast more reviled than revered.

24

Water Problem in South India

Southern India's fast-growing urban areas and its farmers will collide over water allocation unless the government and water users take swift action. Urgently needed are measures that ensure efficient water use in cities and on farms, including regulation of groundwater withdrawal, restoration of traditional rain-collecting reservoirs, and experimentation with different cropping strategies.

In India's arid southern tip, typifies the plight of the country's extensive drylands. Scanty rainfall means residents often must get by on water drawn from small reservoirs and underground sources.

Extended dry periods are punctuated by intense monsoon bursts. When rains lash South India during the monsoons, only a fraction of the downpour is captured for later use. The rivers are seasonal and small compared to the Himalayan cataracts up north.

During the monsoon, these waters swell briefly to gigantic proportions recharging the water tables in their basins and then subside. In times of drought, when the rivers are narrow ribbons, water drawn from below ground sustains crops.

In the cities of South India the problems of water supply are exacerbated by antiquated or non-existent infrastructures that cannot keep up with frenetic growth.

Farmers in South India depend on irrigation to see them through the growing season. They draw their water from three sources: Government canals that bring water from rivers and dams, traditional reservoirs known as "Tanks", and public and private wells often fitted with electric pumps. All three need to be made more efficient.

Besides being enormously expensive, large surface irrigation canals and dams are plagued by massive leaking and evaporation. Tanks collect rain water runoff behind small earthen dams. But these are falling into disrepair as farmers take advantage of low interest government loans and heavily subsidized electricity to switch to private wells fitted with electric pumps. Without maintenance, the tanks fill up with silt and hold less water.

As more wells are dug and as percolation tanks that once recharged underground water supplies fall into disuse, the water table is dropping at a rapid rate.

Farmers who can afford to install powerful electric or diesel pumps on their wells are able to tap the retreating water table, but poorer farmers who raise their water by hand or cattle power from shallow wells often come up dry.

No regulations govern the amount of water a farmer can withdraw from a well, so underground reserves are available on a first-come, first-served basis. Add to this situation electricity rates based on the horsepower of pumps, not on the amount of electricity they consume, and there's no incentive to save water.

Any effort to limit groundwater extraction carries heavy political liabilities. Politicians are reluctant to risk raising theire of farmers, who provide the majority of their votes.

Preventing overdraft where water tables are falling would be a first step toward correcting water troubles. While some areas face the prospect of rationing, others have an abundance of groundwater still to be tapped. Effective legislation must be based on detailed and accurate maps of groundwater supplies—something that doesn't currently exist.

They should also consider instituting higher user fees for its public canal projects and returning to its old policy of charging farmers according to the electricity they consume. Making farmers pay closer to the full price for water and electricity would provide revenue for digging communal wells equipped with electric pumps and overhauling the tank system, while providing an incentive for farmers to conserve.

Using tanks and wells together maximizes the effectiveness of both, since tanks take pressure off groundwater supplies and wells sustain crops during their final weeks of growth when tanks are low. Any efforts to limit the number of new wells dug has to include measures that provide something to those without water, otherwise only those who currently own wells will benefit from groundwater conservation.

Officials might also experiment with encouraging farmers to plant less water-demanding crops such as ragi, sorghum and pulses in place of cotton, sugarcane, bananas and spices.

If politicians act now, they still have a chance to craft measures that are fair rather than desperate. The time is nearing when water for drinking and irrigating crops will have to be culled from careful conservation rather than from the ground.

25

Cheap Transport for India's Millions

Cities congested with cars and buses. Trucks overloaded with goods and passengers. Trains with people clinging to doors and windows in a desperate attempt to get into the crammed interior. These are images of transport in Third World countries which can be observed almost everywhere. Transport is growing at an unprecedented rate: through population growth, through increased mobility of people and the evergrowing trade within and among nations. In most countries, even in the industrialized world, infrastructure is barely able to keep pace with the growth in demand for transportation. Cheap, efficient and environmentally safe transport systems are needed for the movement of people and goods. India, is one of the few developing countries with a well functioning mass transportation system. With the exception of China, no other developing country can boast of a comparable railway network.

140 years of Railway History

Indian Railways are seen by many as a unifying factor in a country which is made up of many different ethnic, cultural and religious groups. Its origions go back to the middle of the last century. The first line was opened in 1853 on a 34 kilometer stretch between Boribunder and Thana near Bombay. In the following year, the first stretch of the Calcutta to Delhi line was opened. Within half a century, a railway system came into being which not only linked the major production centers with the seaports on the Indian Ocean but also crisscrossed the mountainous center of India with its steep mountain ridges, the Western and Eastern Ghats. When India achieved independence from Britain in 1947, most of the present railway network was already in place.

The railways were built by the British not only in order to facilitate internal and external trade, but also for military and strategic reasons in order to be able to rush troops to the borders to protect the Empire or to quell internal unrest. Another reason for creating a mass transport system were the frequent famines which could only be conquered if it was possible to rapidly transport large amounts of food from surplus to deficit areas. The railways thus became an instrument for internal development—contrary to the situation in many African colonies of the time where railways were built with the sole objective of carrying export produce and minerals to the nearest port.

An impediment to efficiency of the Indian Railways was the fact, though, that construction was not planned and implemented by a central authority but by a great number of private companies and governments of India's states. In 1948, when a major effort was made to bring the railways under central control, there were as many as 42 independent railway systems, some very big, some serving only a tiny principality in the central highlands. The situation after independence was made worse through the partition of the former British India into two separate states which disrupted the railway network as it had evolved in the 19th and 20th centuries. In 1951-52, the government regrouped the entire rail network into six railway zones which were later split up further to form the presently existing nine zones. The amalgamation of the railways under one central administration with nine regional centers was the precondition for the necessary standardization of the permanent way, bridges, rolling stock, and equipment.

Standardization was and is a problem for the Indian Railway even more than 47 years after independence. A costly legacy left by the British railway designers are the three different gauges on which trains are running to this day: broad gauge, meter gauge and narrow gauge. Modernization efforts by the railway administration are now concentrated on gradually converting the whole network to broad gauge.

Impressive Achievements

In view of the difficulties faced by the Indian Railways at independence, its development since those days is impressive: in 1950-51, 73 million tons of freight and 1.284 million passengers were carried; these figures rose to 318 million tonnes of freight and 3.858 million passengers in the year 1992-93. These gains were almost entirely achieved through an increase in efficiency.

The rail network grew only slightly at a rate of 1.3 per cent per year.

Modernization also applies to track renewal and electrification of railway lines. Steam engines which are still in use in some parts of the country will be phased out until the turn of the century. The emphasis is on increasing the speed of passenger and freight trains to enlarge the capacity of the existing railway network.

A problem for the modernization programme is the dwindling financial support of the railways through the Indian Government. Whereas allocations for the railways reached a peak of 15.45 per cent of the total budget in the mid-sixties, the share of the railways is now down to 3.4 per cent. The shortfall in investment funds which the railways need to push through their ambitious modernization programme could be made up by mobilizing their own resources if the Railways had the freedom to do their own pricing of services. This however, is not possible. A large part of the freight such as foodgrains and fertilizers has to be carried at highly subsidised rates. Railway managers complain bitterly that the government expects the Railways to carry this "social cost" without funding them adequately to take over this task.

Indian Railways aim at complete self-reliance

In most developing countries, the running of a modern railway network would not be possible without foreign expertise and importation of rolling stock and other hardware. Not so in India. The Railways are almost entirely self-reliant as far as manufacturing their own equipment is concerned. The first steam locomotive was produced in India in 1873. Today, locomotives are produced in two Railway owned factories while the bulk of the passenger coaches are manufactured in the Integrated Coach Factory in Madras. An additional rail coach factory was set up at Kapurthala in 1988 and will produce 1000 coaches after reaching full capacity. Electrical signaling items, railway tracks and other components are also produced in plants belonging to the Railways.

Export of Railway Technology

The high standard of Indian railway expertise is proven by the fact that India is aiding other developing countries in running or modernizing their own railways. The Integrated Coach Factory, for instance, was able to export bogies and coaches to 11 countries in Asia and Africa against stiff Japanese competition.

Indian Railways, thus, can hold its own both as a cheap means of transport for a population of 860 million and as a modern enterprise which produces industrial goods at a high standard. Inspite of the budgetary constraints under which the Railways are working, they manage to maintain a service which is unique in the developing world. It should not be forgotten that rail transport is also environmentally tolerable—a boon in a world which is chocking from the pollution caused by road traffic.

26

Population Growth and Jobs

Since mid-century, the world's labour force has more than doubled—from 1/2 billion people to 2.7 billion, outstripping the growth in job creation. As a result, the United Nations International Labour Organization estimates that nearly 1 billion people, approximately 30 per cent of the global work force, are unemployed or underemployed (working but not earning enough to meet basic needs). Over the next half-century, the world will need to create more than 1.9 billion jobs—all of them in the developing world—just to maintain current levels of employment.

As economists often note, while population growth may boost labour demand (through economic activity and demand for goods), it will most definitely boost labour supply. During the next 50 years, almost 40 million people will enter the global labour force, defined as those between the ages of 15 and 65 seeking work—each year. Between 1995 and 2050, some 1.9 billion additional jobs will need to be created to absorb these new would-be workers. The most pressing needs will be found in the world's poorest nations—a sobering example of the vicious cycle linking poverty and population growth.

As the children of today represent the workers of tomorrow, the interaction between population growth and jobs is most acute in nations with young populations. Nations such as Peru, Mexico, Indonesia, and Zambia with more than half their population below the age of 25 will feel the burden of this labour flood. In the Middle East and Africa, 40 per cent of the population is under the age of 15. Since new entrants into the labour force were born at least 15 years ago, measures to reduce population growth have a delayed effect on the growth of the labour force, highlighting the urgency of taking action on population.

Nowhere is the employment challenge greater than in Africa, where at least 40 per cent of the population lives in absolute poverty. Although 8 million people entered the sub-Saharan work force in 1997, by 2030 this resource-scarce region will have to absorb more than 17 million new entrants each year. Over the next half-century, Nigeria's labour force is projected to grow by 246 per cent and Ethiopia's will soar by 337 per cent—both faster than growth of the general population. At current growth rates, the size of the labour force in sub-Saharan Africa will more than triple by 2050.

As a result of unprecedented population growth and increasing acceptance of female participation in the work force, the number of people seeking jobs in the Middle East and North Africa, a region already plagued by double-digit unemployment rates, will double in the next 50 years. In Algeria, where unemployment stands at 22 per cent, the labour force is growing at a staggering 4.2 per cent annually, and the number seeking work will more than double by 2050. Egypt alone will need to create 26 million more jobs by 2050 as its total population hits 115 million.

Nations throughout Asia will also see phenomenal increases in the number seeking work, including Pakistan, where the work force will grow from 70 million in 1998 to 205 million by 2050. Over the next 25 years, India will add nearly 10 million to its work force each year. During the same period, China will add nearly 6 million annually due to population growth alone, compounding the work short-ages causes by the current flood of migrants to China's coastal cities and by massive layoffs—estimated at more than 30 million—as state-run operations are scaled back.

Nations are hard-pressed to educate and train rapidly growing numbers of young people in marketable skills for the global workplace. Moreover, meeting the basic needs of a growing population draws scarce foreign exchange and other resources from investments in education and job creation. Throughout the world, young people entering the work force are increasingly faced with unemployment and social marginalization. In most societies, unemployment rates for those under 25 are substantially higher than for older people.

Surplus farmland once served as a traditional source of employment for growing populations, as new land could be plowed to generate work and income. However, global per capita Greenland has dropped by half and considerably more in certain nations since 1950. Moreover, the mechanization of agriculture fuels the exodus of job seekers into the world's urban areas, where unemployment is often most acute heavily reliant on natural capital in the past, future job creation will require massive amount of financial capital to jump-start the industrial and service sectors.

As the balance between the demand and supply of labour is tipped by population growth, wages—the price of labour—tend to decrease. And in a situation of labour surplus, the quality of jobs may not improve as fast for workers will settle for longer hours, fewer benefits and less control over work activities.

Employment is the key to obtaining food, housing, health services, and education, in addition to providing self-respect and self-fulfillment. Rising numbers of unemployed people could drive global poverty and hunger to precarious levels, fueling political instability.

27

Population Growth and Income

Global economic output, the total of all goods, and services produced, grew from $5 trillion in 1950 to $29 trillion in 1998, expanding more than twice as fast as population. This increase of nearly sixfold boosted incomes rather substantially for most of humanity. Growth of the world economy from 1990 to 1997 exceeded the growth during the 10,000 years from the beginning of agriculture until 1950.

Economic output per person climbed from just over @1,900 in 1950 to nearly @5,000 in 1997, a gain of 163 per cent. Although there is an enormous income gap between industrial and developing countries, the latter's economies are growing far more rapidly. Growth in industrial countries has slowed to scarcely 2 per cent a year during the 1990s, compared with nearly 6 per cent a year in developing nations.

The faster-growing region in the world from 1990 to 1997 was Asia, which averaged nearly 8 per cent annually. This growth was led by China, whose economy has been increasing at nearly 10 per cent a year throughout much of this decade, making it the world's fastest-growing economy. Since 1980, China's economic output has doubled every eight years.

Incomes have risen most rapidly in developing countries where population growth has slowed the most, including, importantly, the countries of East Asia—South Korea, Taiwan, China, Thailand, Indonesia, and Malaysia, Concentrating early on reducing birth rates helped to boost savings to invest in education, health care, and the infrastructure needed by a modern industrial society.

At the other end of the spectrum, African countries—largely ignoring family planning-have been overwhelmed by the sheer number of young people who need to be educated and employed. With population growth rates remaining at close to 3 per cent or more a year, most of any economic growth that occurred has been absorbed by the increasing population, leaving little to raise incomes.

The enormous growth during the 1990s, particularly in East Asia, is due to the huge increase in private capital flows into developing countries. Between 1990 and 1997, annual private capital flows increased from $42 billion to $256 billion, a gain of more than six fold. This substantial amount of money dwarfs traditional flows in public funds under international aid programmes.

Although incomes in much of the developing world are rising rapidly, they are not rising for everyone. The World Bank estimates that 1.3 billion of the world's people subsist on $1 a day or less. For this one fifth of humanity, trapped at a subhuman level of existence, there has not been any meaningful progress.

The sources of growth are changing. In earlier times, most of the growth was in agriculture. Since the advent of the Industrial Revolution, however, more and more of the growth has been concentrated in industry. Then beginning around mid-century, the services sector-insurance, banking, education-began to expand rapidly, accounting for most of the change in the industrial world. More recently, growth has been concentrated in the information sector as computerization of the economy and telecommunications have grown at extraordinary rates.

The good news is that the global economy has been expanding at a near record pace during the 1990s. The bad news is that the economy, as now structured, is outgrowing the Earth's eco system. The result is excessive pressures on the natural systems and resources. As noted in the first section of this paper, from 1950 to 1997 the use of lumber more than doubled. That of paper increased six fold, the fish catch increased nearly five fold, grain consumption nearly tripled, fossil fuel burning nearly quandrupled, and air and water pollutants multiplied several fold. The unfortunate reality is that the economy continues to expand, but the eco system on which it depends does not, creating an increasingly stressed relationship.

If the economy were to expand only enough to cover population growth until 2050, it would need to grow from the $29 trillion of 1997 to $47 trillion. This, of course, would merely maintain current incomes, unacceptable though they are for much of humanity. If, on the other hand, the economy were to continue to expand at 3 per cent per year, global economic output would reach $138 trillion in the year 2050.

Even the first, more modest, growth projection would likely lead to a deterioration of the Earth's natural systems to the point where the economy itself would begin to decline. It is easy to foresee a scenario of continuing forest destruction, aquifer depletion, and eco system collapse that would lead to economic decline. If the world cannot simultaneously convert the economy to one that is environmentally sustainable—one that does not destroy its own support systems—and move to a lower population trajectory, economic decline will be hard to avoid.

28

Population Growth and Housing

Over the past half-century, the world's housing stock has grown roughly in step with population. Yet for more and more people worldwide, adequate and affordable housing remains beyond reach, driving some into substandard dwellings and slums and others onto the street. This situation stands to worsen, for the need for housing worldwide is projected to nearly double over the next 50 years.

Although industrial nations currently occupy a disproportionately large share of the world's households relative to their population, virtually all future growth will occur in developing countries, where housing requirements will more than double by the middle of the twenty-first century. This phenomenal growth results from the potent synergy between population growth and a shift toward fewer people per household—a trend that is especially pronounced where economic growth is rapid.

HABITAT, the United Nations Centre for Human Settlements, has projected housing requirements based on roughly a 30 per cent reduction in people per household over the next 50 years.

These figures are purely statistical estimates and do not consider possible checks in housing growth, such as materials or financial constraints, intensified land competition, or increased poverty. Our own projections assume that household size will indeed decrease, as fertility rates drop and as extended families become more rare, but by a more modest 15 per cent.

Over the next 50 years, housing needs in Africa and the Middle East are expected to increase more than thre efold, with tremendous gains in the region's most populous nations; demands are to increase 3.5 times in Nigeria and 4.5 times in Ethiopia. Although less dramatic percentage increases are expected in Asia, the doubling of households in the region will require nearly 700 million additional homes by 2050. Still, some countries there, such as Pakistan and neighboring Afghanistan, will see housing needs increase nearly three and a half times.

The projected growth in housing needs becomes all the more daunting given that rapid population growth—combined with rapid urban growth—has already left a large share of the world's population without adequate housing. HABITAT estimates that at least 600 million urban dwellers and more than 1 billion rural dwellers in Africa, Asia, and Latin America live in housing that is so over crowded and of such poor quality with such inadequate provision for water, sanitation, drainage, and garbage collection that their lives and their health are continually at risk.

As the supply of housing falls behind demand, the quality of available housing tends to deteriorate. Cheaper, less durable materials, such as scrap metal and cardboard, are substituted for more expensive, weather-resistant materials, such as concrete and wood. Fierce competition in swelling urban areas for desirable land can eliminate all hope of low-income households acquiring a plot for housing. As choice of location dwindles, shanty towns and other low-quality settlements develop on marginal land ill suited for housing-in floodplains, on steep hillsides, near garbage dumps or other environmentally risky sites. From New York to Beijing, cities are faced with land and materials constraints even as their populations continue to grow.

At the same time, housing area per person continues to increase in certain nations and among the more affluent segments of other nations, placing additional stress on prime space and building materials. In the United States, Western Europe, and Japan—a nation traditionally known for small dwellings—floor space per person has more than doubled in new single family homes since mid-century. The global disparity in floor space per person-Washington, D.C.., at the high end with 70 square meters per person, and most of humanity at around 9 square meters per person-will likely mimic the growing global disparity in income, as wealthy households scale up and poorer households fill up.

Housing can provide a connection to a supply of fresh water and sanitation facilities. But as its quality deteriorates, so do these basic amenities. Half the world's people are without access to sanitation and nearly this many 2.7 billion—are without a reliable source of safe drinking water. Shortages of housing that provides these basic services are most acute in cities, where rapid urbanization and high population densities place heightened demands on infrastructure. And still housing needs are projected to soar in the regions of the world where access to water and sanitation are most constrained.

The ultimate manifestation of population growth outstripping the supply of housing is homelessness. The United Nations estimates that at least 100 million of the world's people—roughly the same as the population of Mexico have no home; the number tops 1 billion if those with especially insecure or temporary accommodations, such as squatters, are included. In many developing countries, squatter communities are home to 30-60 per cent of the urban population. There are some 250,000 pavement dwellers in Bombay alone. Human who are born, live, and die in the streets—are common in all major cities. Unless the world moves to a lower population trajectory, the ranks of homeless are likely to swell dramatically.

29

Population Growth and Grain Production

The relationship between the growth in world population and the grain harvest has shifted over the last half-century, neatly dividing this period into two distinct eras. From 1950 to 1984, growth and the grain harvest easily exceeded that of population, raising the harvest per person from 247 kilograms to 342, a grain of 38 per cent. During the 14 years since then, growth in the grain harvest has fallen behind that of population, dropping output per person from its historic high in 1984 to an estimated 317 kilograms in 1998—a decline of 7 per cent, or 0.5 per cent a year.

These global trends conceal widely divergent developments among countries, contrasts that can be seen for the world's two most populous nations: India and China. In both, grain production per person was close to 200 kilograms as recently as 1978. Since then, the figure in India has edge up slightly but still falls short of 200 kilograms, while in china production has surged since the economic reforms in 1978, with per-person output now at nearly 300 kilograms. The combination of a dramatic surge in grain production and an equally dramatic reduction in **population growth** has given China a large margin of safety, effectively eliminating most of its hunger and malnutrition. Meanwhile, although India has also achieved impressive gains in its harvest, these have been largely cancelled by population growth, leaving its 976 million people living close to the margin.

What has happened in China and India is the story of developing countries in general. The overwhelming majority have achieved substantial, if not dramatic, grains in their grain harvests over the last half-century. Some, such as Thailand, have combined this with a much slower growth of population, which means that agricultural grains translate into rising grain production per person. In Pakistan, by contrast, grain production per person climbed steadily for awhile, but it peaked in 1981 at 186 kilograms. Since then it has been declining nearly 1 per cent a year. In effect, Pakistan's farmers are losing the battle with population growth.

The slower growth in the world grain harvest since 1984 is due to the lack of new land and to slower growth in irrigation and fertilizer use. Irrigated area per person, after expanding by 4 per cent since then as growth in the irrigated area has fallen behind that of population.

The increase in world fertilizer use has slowed dramatically since 1990, as diminishing returns to the application of additional fertilizer has stabilized use in the United States, Western Europe, and Japan and slowed annual growth in world fertilizer use from 6 per cent between 1950 and 1990 to scarcely 2 per cent in recent years.

Although Malthus was primarily concerned with the additional demand for grain generated by population growth, rising affluence is also playing a role. In a low income country such as India, grain consumption per person is less than 200 kilograms per year and diets are typically dominated by a single starchy staple-rice, for instance. With scarcely a pound of grain available a day per person, nearly all must be consumed directly, leaving little for conversion into animal protein. For the average American, on the other hand, the great bulk of the 800 kilogram daily grain consumption is taken in indirectly in the form of beef, pork, poultry, eggs, milk, cheese, ice cream, and yogurt. At the intermediate level, in a country like Italy, people consume 400 kilograms of grain a day. Future food price stability thus depends on expanding production fast enough to keep up with both population growth and rising affluence.

One question often asked is, How many people can the Earth support? This must be answered with another question, at what level of consumption? If the world grain harvest of 1.87 billion tons were expanded to 2 billion tons in the years ahead, it would support 10 billion Indians or 2.5 billion Americans. To answer the question of how many people the Earth can support, we first have to know the level of consumption we expect to live at.

Now that the frontiers of agricultural settlement have disappeared, future growth in grain production must come almost entirely from raising land productivity. Unfortunately, this is becoming more difficult. After rising at 2.1 per cent a year from 1950 to 1990, the annual increase in rainland productivity dropped to scarcely 1 per cent from 1990 to 1997. The challenge for the world's farmers is to reverse this decline at a time when cropland area per person is dropping, and the crop yield response to additional fertilizer use is falling.

Bibliography

BOOKS

Ajit, K. Dandar, Studies on Rural Development Experience and Issues, Inter India Publications, Delhi, 1984•

Amal Ray and Vanitha Venkata Subbaiah, Studies in Rural Development Administration, World Press, Calcutta, 1984•

Appaswamy, Legal effects on Social Reforms, Madras Christian Literature Society, Madras, 1929•

Arora, R.C., Integrated Rural Development, S•Chand and Company Ltd•, New Delhi, 1979•

Azad, R.N., Integrated Rural Development, S• Chand and Company Ltd•, New Delhi, 1979•

Aziz, Sartaz., Rural Development Learning from China, London, Mc Millan Press Ltd•, Madras, 1978•

Balaramulu, C.H., Administration of Anti Poverty Programmes, A Study of SFDA, Ashok Printers, Warangal, 1984•

Bandyopadhyay, J•, The Poverty of Nations, Allied Publishers Pvt•, Ltd•, 1988•

Bardhan, P.K., Poverty and Trickle down in Rural India; Oxford University Press, 1986•

Bhatt, G.D., An Evaluation of IRDP: Rural Development Programmes in India, Shanthi Publishers, New Delhi, 1990•

Bajaj, J.L., and Sastri, C., Rural Poverty; Issues and Options, Print House, Luckhnow, 1985.

Bhatia, B.M., Poverty, Agriculture and Economic Growth, Vikas Publishers, New Delhi, 1977.

Bhattacharya, S., Rural Poverty in India, Ashish Publishing House, New Delhi, 1989.

Chadha, G.K., The State and Rural Economic Transformation, Sage Publications, New Delhi, 1986.

Chowdhry, D. Paul., New Partnership in Rural Development, M.M., Publishers, New Delhi, 1978.

Dandekar V.M. and Rath, N., Poverty in India, Published by Indian School of Political Economy, Pune, 1971.

Daljit Singh Dhillon, Integrated Rural Development, Vohra Publishers and Distributors, Allied Publications, New Delhi, 1983.

Das Gupta, Biplab, Rural Development–The CADC Experience, Comprehensive Area Development Cooperation, Calcutta, 1982.

Dat, T.M., Social Inequalities and Rural Development, National Publishing House, Bombay, 1988.

Desai, B.M., (ed), Interaction for Rural Development, Indian Institute of Management, Ahmadabad, 1986.

Dantawala, M.L., Poverty Alleviation Through Rural Development in Administrative Arrangements for Rural Development–A Perspective, Sponsored by the Planning Commission and Department of Rural Development, Government of India, NIRD, Hyderabad, 1985.

Dhingra, I.C., Rural Economics, S. Chand and Company New Delhi, 1987.

Dubhashi, R. R., Rural Development Administration in India, Popular Prakashan Publishers, Bombay, 1970.

Eleanor Zelliot, The Untouchables ib Contemporary India, University of Arizona Press, Tuscon, 1972.

Franida, Marcus, Indias Rural Development, An Assessment of alternatives, Indian University Press, Bloomington, 1979.

Gadgil, D.R., District Development Planning, Asian Publishing House, Bombay, 1967.

Galbraith, J.K., The Nature of Mass Poverty, Penguin Books, 1984.

Girippa Somu, Income, Saving and Investment Pattern in Rural India, Ashish Publication House, New Delhi, 1985.

Gupta, S.C., Development Banking for Rural Development, Deep & Deep Publications, New Delhi, 1987.

Herendra, J.M., Rural Development and Social Change in Non-formal Education, Manohara Book Services, New Delhi, 1977.

Hirway Indira, Abolition of Poverty in India, Vikas Publishing House, New Delhi, 1986.

Hough, Cooperative Movement in India, Calcutta, Oxford University Press, 1979.

Indian Bankers, Role of Banks in Village Life, Financing Growth Centres for Rural Development, I.B.A., Bombay, 1977.

Issac, H.R., Indias Ex-untouchables, Asia Publishing House, Bombay, 1965.

Jain, S.C., Rural Development Institutions and Strategies, Rawat Publications, Jaipur, 1985.

Jain, S. P., Economic Institutions and Rural Uplift, Popular Prakashan, Bombay, 1988.

Khan, A.R., Institutional Finance for Rural Development: Comparitive Study of India and Bangladesh, Ph. D. Thesis (unpublished) Gokhale Institute of Politics and Economics, Pune, 1983.

Khatkar, R.K., and Nandal, D. S., Impact of Rural Financing by Regional Rural Banks to the Rural Poor in Bhiwani district of Haryana, Abhinava Publications, New Delhi, 1977.

Lahiri, T.B., Rural Development: A short Ter, Strategy, Jayashree Prakasham Publishers, Calcutta, 1980.

Lakshminarayana, H.D., Studies in Rural Development, S.V., University, Tirupati, 1970.

Leela, Uma, Design of Rural Development, Lessons for Africa, The Johns Hopkins University Press, Balti More, London, 1975.

Madan, G.R., Indian Social Problems, Allied Publications, Bombay, 1975.

Madhuker, V. Namjoshi, Planning for Weaker Sections, Centre for Studies in Social Service, Pune, 1978.

Mahajan, R.K., Differential Gains of IRDP, Concept Publishing Company, New Delhi, 1991.

Mayor. A.C., Castes and Kinship in Central India, Routledge and Kegan Paul, London.

Maheswari, S. R., Rural Development in India, Sage Publications Pvt. Ltd., New Delhi 1984.

Mishra, S.D., Integrated Rural Development Programme–A Direct Assault on Poverty, Ashish Publishers, New Delhi, 1986.

Mishra, R.P. and Sarma, K.P., Problems and Prospects of Rural Development in India, Heritage Publications, New Delhi, 1980.

Moddie, A.P., Approaches to Rural Development, Allied Publishers, Bombay, 1974.

Mumtaz Alikhan, Scheduled Castes and their Status in India, Uppal Publishing House, New Delhi, 1980.

Naidu, M.C., Financing of IRDP in India, Discovery Publishing House, New Delhi, 1991.

Naidu, L.K., Bank Finance and Rural Development, Ashish Publishing House, New Delhi, 1985.

Narayana, D.L., Studies in Rural Development, S.V. University, Tirupati, 1968.

NIRD, Rural Development in India, Some Facets, NIRD Publications, Hyderabad, 1987.

Padhy Kishore Chandra, Rural Development in Modern India, B.R. Publishing Corporation, New Delhi, 1986.

Patel, A.R., Integrated Rural Development and Institutional Finance, Commerce Publications Ltd., Bombay, 1982.

Pauline Kolenda, Caste in Contemporary India, Jaipur Rewat Publications, 1983.

Paul Samuel, Strategic Management of Development, Programmes Guidelines for action, I.L.O. Publications, Geneva, 1983.

Ramachandran, H., Village Clusters and Rural Development, Concept Publishing Company, New Delhi, 1986.

Rao, R.V., Rural Institutionalisation in India, Concept Publishing Co., New Delhi, 1976.

Rao, V.M., Rural Development and the Village, Sterling Publishers, New Delhi, 1980.

Sha, S.M., Rural Development Planning and Reforms, Abhinav Publications, New Delhi, 1977.

Sharma, S.K. and Malhotra, S.L., Integrated Rural Development: Approach, Strategy and Perspectives, Abhinav Publications, New Delhi, 1977.

Srivastava, A.K., Integrated Rural Development Programme in India: Policy and Administration, Deep & Deep Publications, New Delhi, 1986.

Srivastava, U.K., and George, P.S., Rural Development in Action, Somayya Publications, Bombay, 1977.

Sundaram, I.S., Anti-Poverty Rural Development in India, D.K., Publishers, New Delhi, 1984.

Thimmaiah, G., Studies in Rural Development, Chugh Publications, Allahabad, 1973.

Upadhyaya, R., Integrated Rural Development in India–Basic Approach in Policy, Himalaya Publishing House, Bombay, 1989.

Vasudeva Rao, D., Facts of Rural Development in India, Ashish Publishing House, New Delhi, 1985.

Vivekananda Rao, V.K.R.V., Planning Unit Areas for Integrated Rural Development: Studies in Integrated Rural Development–An Exercise, Ashish Publishing House, New Delhi, 1986.

PERIODICALS

Ahluwalia, M.S., Rural Poverty and Agricultural Performance in India, Journal of Development Studies, April, 1978.

Alexander, K.C., and Naidu, N.Y., Flow of Credit and Subsidy under IRDP in Madhya Pradesh, Journal of Rural Development, 3(5), 1985, pp. 415-450.

Ammaniah, K.K., Alleviation of Poverty in India: Need for a New Growth Strategies, Economic Review, Monthly Economic Journal of Syndicate Bank, Vol. 27, No. 11, June 1982.

Bagchee Sandeep, Poverty Alleviation Programmes in the Seventh Plan an Appraisal, Economic and Political Weekly, Vol., XXII, No. 4, January, 1987.

Balakrishna, S. et, al., Monitoring of IRDP, A Study in Warangal District of Andhra Pradesh, Journal of Rural Development, 3(1) 1984, pp. 1-22.

Balakrishna, S., Incidence of Rural Poverty in Recent Years, Behavioural Science and Rural Development Vol. III, No. 1, 1980, p.10.

Bala Subramaniam, N.S., Seventh Plan and Rural Development, Kurukshetra, Vol. XXXIII, No. 1, October, 1984, pp. 51-53.

Balishter and Singham Roshan, IRDP Financing by State Bank of India, Financing Agriculture, 16(3) July-September, 1984, pp. 10-16.

Bandyopadyaya, R., Regional Development and Credit Plan, Prajanan, Vol. I, No. 2, April-June, 1972, pp. 115-140.

Bhatt, G.D., From Community Development to Integrated Rural Development, Kurukshetra, Vol. XXXVI. No. 9, June, 1988, pp.27-30.

Bhargavan, B.S., Need for an Effective Evaluation in Rural Development, Kurukshetra, Vol. XXXII, No. 10, July 1984, pp. 51-53.

Biswarth Gosh, Challenges of Poverty Removal, Yojana, Vol. 30, October, 1986, pp. 4–6.

Chandra Karete, M.S., Tardy Implementation of IRDP, Yojana, Vol. XXXIX, No. 10 October, 1985, p. 13.

Chandra Sekhar Rao, K. and Naidu, V.J., Employment Generation under IRDP, A study, Kurukshetra, Vol. XXXIV, No. 9, June, 1988, pp.20.

Chaturvedi, Y.S., Naidu, K. and Sridhar, M.J., Beneficiaries of IRDP in Gujarath, and Rajasthan–A Study, Kurukshetra, Vol. XXXVI, No. 12, September, 1988, pp. 25-28.

Chinna Swamy Naidu, M. and Amarnath Naidu, D., Working of IRDP and Financial Institutions: A Study, Kurukshetra, Vol. XXXVI, No. 12, September, 1988, pp. 15-16.

Das, H.C.L., Rural Development Planning in Bihar, A Case Study of IRDP, Indian Journal of Agricultural Economics Vol. XXXIX, No. 3, July–September, 1984, pp. 479-480.

Das Gupta, et. al., Problems of Rural Poverty, A Sociological Exposure; Economic Studies, Vol. XXI, No. I, July 1980, pp. 33-47.

Dhillan, D.S., and Sandhu, N.S., Integrated Rural Development Programme, An Over View, Kurukshetra, Vol. XXXVI, No. 12, September, 1988, pp. 10-14.

George, K.M., Rural Development Programmes, its Strength and Weaknesses, Indian Journal of Agricultural Economics, Vol. XXXIX, No. 3, September, 1984, pp. 266-275.

Hanumantha Rao, C.H., Rural Society and Agricultural Development; Case of India–Economic and Political Weekly, Vol., XXVI, No. 11 and 12, 1991.

Jacob, S. Thudipara, Training for IRDP functionaires; An Over View, Kurukshetra, Vol. XXXIX, No. 9, June, 1991, pp. 25-27.

Joshi, V.H., Rural Poverty in the Third World, A Relative Perception, Southern Economist, Vol. XXIII, No. 1, May, 1984, p. 24.

Khanna Sandeep, Managing IRDP Approach, Yojana, Vol. 28, No. 14, March, 1984, p. 24.

Krishnan Kutty, A.C., A Case Study of IRDP in Kerala Village, Indian Journal of Agricultural Economics, September, 1985.

Kurien, N.J., IRDP, How relevant is it, Economic and Poliical Weekly, Vol. XXII, No. 52, December, 1987, p. 561.

Malayadri, P., Success of IRDP, Myth and reality; A study, Kurukshetra, 33(11) 1985.

Mary, A. Arul, Flows and Monitoring for IRDP, Journal of Rural Development 3(1) 1984, pp. 23-28.

Mohanan Sundaram, V., How IRDP schemes can be better implemented Kurukshetra, Vol. XXXIV, No. 12, September, 1988, pp. 4–9.

Mohinder Singh, Coordination under IRDP, A Study, Kurukshetra, Vol. XXXVI, No. 12, September 1988, pp. 29-32.

Nadeem Mohsin and Raghunath Jha, Regional Rural Banks and IRDP, Yojana, Vol. 31, No. 13, July 1987, pp. 10-12.

Neeta Gautam and Singh, D.V., Working of IRDP in Himachal Pradesh, A Case Study, Kurukshetra, Vol. XXXIX, No. 9, June, 1991, pp. 28-29.

Perumalla Rao, D. and Natarajan, R., IRDP Assistance in Andhra Pradesh: An Evaluation, Kurukshetra, Vol. XXXIV No. 6, March, 1988, pp. 25-29.

Raghumath Jha, What Ails IRDP, Yojana, Vol. 30, No. 16. September, 1986, pp. 18-20.

Ramaiah, P. Veeravenkataiah and Mohan Reddy, Impact of IRDP on Rural Poor, A Micro Study, Kurukshetra, Vol. XXXVI, No. 12 September, 1988, pp. 19-22.

Rao, V.K.R.V., Integrated Rural Development Southern Economist, Vol. 16, No. 14, November, 1977, pp. 9-11.

Rath, Neelakantha, Garib Hatao, Can IRDP Do It, Economic Political Weekly, Vol. XX, No. 13, March, 1985.

Santhra, S.K. and Mondal S., Integrated Rural Development Programme; Problems and Prospects, Kurukshetra, Vol. XXXVI, No. 12, September, 1988, pp. 23-24.

Sarkar, D.C., Organising IRDP beneficiaries, Kurushetra, Vol. XXXVI, No. 6. March, 1988, pp. 30-31.

Sharma, P.N., IRDP and Poverty Alleviation Strategies, An Appraisal, Kurukshetra, Vol. XXXVI, No. 6, March, 1988, pp. 17-22.

Shivaiah, M. IRDP, Alleviation of Poverty and Block Administration, Organisation Support for improving performance, NIRD, Hyderabad, 1984.

Stepletion Thomas, General Speech on Approaches to Integrated Rural Development in 63rd Science Congress, Waltair, 1976.

Thaha, M., et. al., Flow of Credit and Subsidy Under IRDP in Orissa, Journal of Rural Development 6(5) 1987, pp. 450-467.

Tripathy, R.N., Flow of credit and subsidy under IRDP, Journal of Rural Development 3(5), September, 1985, pp. 373-396.

Umesh Samuel, A. and Paul Ray, S., Role of Officials and People Participation in Rural Development Schemes, Kurukshetra, Vol. XXXIX, No. 8, May, 1991, pp. 9-13.

Varma, M.V., IRDP in Bihar, Planning and Implementation, the Economic Times, 13(286), January, 1987, pp. 9-16.

Vashist, P.D., Monitoring System at National and State level for Rural Development, Kurukshetra, Vol. XXXVI, No. 6, March, 1988, pp. 23-24.

REPORTS

District Rural Development Agency–The Annual Action Plans of DRDA, IRDP, 1980-81–1990-91.

District Rural Development Agency–The Report of DRDA, TRYSEM, 1980-81–1990-91.

District Rural Development Agency–The Report of the DRDA, PASMA, 1983-84–1989-90.

District Rural Development–The Report of DRDA, DWACRA 1989-90.

District Rural Development–The Report of DRDA, NRDP, 1980-81–1985-86.

Food and Agricultural Organisation–Report on World Conference on Agrarian Reforms and Rural Development, Rome, 1979.

Government of Andhra Pradesh–Andhra Pradesh Statistical Abstracts, 1981 and 1982, Bureau of Economics and Statistics, Hyderabad.

Government of India–All India Rural Credit Survey, Report of the Committee of the Director A.D., Gorwala, Bombay, Reserve Bank of India, 1954.

Government of India–All India Debt and Investment Survey, 1971-72, Bombay, RBI, 1977.

Government of India–Concurrent Evaluation of IRDP, The Main Findings of the Survey for October 1985-June, 1986, Department of Rural Development, New Delhi, Ministry of Agriculture, 1986.

Government of India–Concurrent Evaluation of IRDP, The Main Findings of the Survey for January-December 1987, Department of Rural Development, New Delhi, Ministry of Agriculture, 1988.

Government of India–Evaluation Report on IRDP, New Delhi, Planning Evaluation Organisation, Planning Commission, May, 1985.

Government of India–IRDP and Allied Programmes like TRYSEM, DWACRA in Rural Areas. A Manual, Department of Rural Development, New Delhi, Ministry of Agriculture, July, 1987.

Government of India–Report of the Committee to Review Arrangements for Institutional Credit for Agriculture and Rural Development (CRAFICARD), Bombay, RBI, 1981.

Government of India–Report of the Committee to Review the Existing Administrative Arrangements for Rural Development and Poverty Alleviation Programme (CAARD), Department of Rural Development, Ministry of Agriculture, December, 1985.

Government of India–First Five Year Plan 1951-56.

Government of India–Second Five Year Plan 1956-61.

Government of India–Third Five Year Plan 1961-66.

Government of India–Annual Plan, 1966-69.

Government of India–Fourth Five Year Plan, 1970-74.

Government of India–Fifth Five Year Plan, 1974-78.

Government of India–Sixth Five Year Plan, 1980-85.

Government of India–Seventh Five Year Plan, 1985-90.

IFMR–An Economic Assessment of Poverty Eradication and Rural Unemployment Alleviation Programme and their Prospects Madras, 1984.

ICSSR–An Evaluation of IRDP, Centre for Research, Planning and Action, New Delhi, 1984.

NABARD–Study of Implementation of IRDP, Bombay, 1987.

SBI–A study of IRDP in 10 lead Districts in India, 1984.

World Bank–The World Development Report, 1990.

JOURNALS

Economic and Political Weekly, Bombay.

Indian Economic Journal, Bombay.

Indian Journal of Agricultural Economics, Bombay.

Journal of Development Studies, Washington.

Journal of Rural Development, Hyderabad.

Kurukshetra, New Delhi.

Pigmy Economic Review, Manipal.

Prajan, Bombay.

Southern Economist, Bangalore.

The Economic Times, Bombay.

The Hindu, Madras.

Yojana, Delhi.